Author: Felix Hahlbrock Ponce, Berlin (Germany)

Italo-Western and more...

A filmic guide

Felix Hahlbrock Ponce

Index

Annex:

Introduction

From the beginning of the seventh art, the western was one of the most recurrent genres in its country of origin. The United States, as a nation, bases its existential foundations on the expansion from the colonies on the Atlantic coast towards the west. The events of the 19th century in North America would give rise to numerous adventure stories set in the inhospitable regions of the still young and rapidly growing country. The Anglos, and other Euro-descendants, displaced the native Indians, settling towards western areas and discovering gold mines to exploit, which provided them with increasingly lucrative economic resources.

In this historical context, that of a new country in gestation, there were immense territories to be explored, lawless areas and numerous dangers lurking. In other words, adventure was at hand. Arid villages in the middle of the desert served as the stage for all-out fighting between whites and Indians, between cruel outlaws and lawkeepers; or for rivalries between rough and taciturn bounty hunters and self-sacrificing sheriffs. That era was not yet so far back in time when the film industry began its journey, at the end of the 19th century.

The American western launched great icons like filmmaker John Ford, or his namesake actor John Wayne, into stardom. The success of these films also reverberated in Europe. From the 1960s onwards, it was the Italians in particular who revived and renewed the western genre. Sergio Leone, specially, brought out true masterpieces. His Dollar Trilogy, which brought fame to the famous Clint Eastwood, caused such a sensation that in the following years the "spaghetti-western" trend would develop (as the sub-genre was vulgary and somewhat disdainfully known). Leone, Eastwood and Morricone (direction, acting and music, respectively) are the most prominent names in this European appendix of "cowboy" cinema set in the "wild west" but shot in the Old Continent.

As is widely known, most of the Italian westerns were filmed in Spain, specifically in the Tabernas desert in Almería. In fact, several Italian westerns are actually Spanish/Italian co-productions.

The Italian-style western, whose pioneers had been Leone and Corbucci, would become even more popular than the original American western in some respects. For it was more violent, more raw, more direct, with less dialogue and more visual power, without so much idealization, without a clear distinction between good and evil. In other words: more realistic. For in the "Wild West", as its name suggests, there was not much room for scruples.

At this point, it is interesting to bring up the parallelism between the western genre and the chambara, the Japanese samurai films. Most of the time, both the stories and the atmosphere are perfectly extrapolated. This was understood from the very beginning by the great Sergio Leone, who with "For a Fistful of Dollars" (the starting point of the Italo-Western) made an apocryphal remake of Akira Kurosawa's "Yojimbo" (which would cost him a lawsuit by the Japanese director). Both the western and the chambara are usually set at the same time, around the 1960s and 1970s. Interestingly, that was the time when traditional Japan was collapsing in the East (with the decline of the Tokugawa shogunate) while the US was being forged as a continental power in the West.

There are undeniable similarities between the Western and the Chambara. These genres would inspire each other, feeding off each other, as they were both two visions (one Eastern and one Western) of the same archetypes. The bounty hunter, a lone gunman with few words, has the same role and characteristics in Westerns as the ronin wanderer who makes his way through the Chambara films with his katana.

In this book you will find reviewed several of the most emblematic Italo-Western films. From the classics of Leone or Corbucci to lesser-known feature films, which, without matching the works of the masters, follow the storylines and stylistic patterns of the sub-genre, sometimes contributing some innovations.

In addition, we include as an appendix some western films that, without being Italian, have the same patterns of "spaghetti-western" (i.e.: amorality, violence, black humor...). Among those other films included in this guide, a special mention deserves "El Topo" by Alejandro Jodorowsky, which, besides being formally a western (clearly inspired by the Italian style), has a deep mystical-initiatic content. In the appendix there are also some Mexican western films, which emerged from the great popularity of the genre (revived by the Italians). These Mexican westerns, which used to be shot on a shoestring budget, were several times crossovers with other genres such as horror, and even with the typically Mexican genre of wrestling. The cinematographic quality (according to the criteria of the purists) was usually not very high, but in many occasions these films were of great interest precisely because of their bizarre characteristics.

The purpose of this book is to serve as a guide for Italo-Western fans, compiling the most important and famous films of the subgenre, and including, as a curiosity, others that are less known or that, without being strictly Italo-Western, have similarities with that kind of cinema in terms of stories and style.

Some of the following reviews have already appeared on the blog Alucine Cinéfago or on the website "Nocreasnada", while most are unpublished so far.

Felix Hahlbrock Ponce

About the author

Felix Hahlbrock Ponce (born 1985) is the author of the Spanish blog Alucine Cinéfago. In this space, the autodidactic German-Spanish critic has been publishing reviews and analyses of various films since June 2015 - focusing mainly on the genres of horror, suspense and crime, as well as their respective variants.

He has written a book on Narciso Ibáñez Serrador's "Historias para no dormir", which has been reviewed by the website Fantástico Español. He also published "Shintaro Katsu´s Zatoichi", about the film saga starred by the Japanese blind swordsman Zatoichi, as well as "The Lone Wolf and Cub... and other samurai stories of cinema and television". He also published a compilation book with reviews of each and every one of the more than 50 films of the heroic fighter "Santo, the Silver Masked Man". He also dedicated a volume to the

Colombian television series "Escobar: the Patron of Evil," about drug trafficker Pablo Escobar. These books have been translated into English (except for "Las Historias para no dormir" and Pablo Escobar's), and are available on Amazon in both paper and e-book versions.

In Alucine Cinéfago, cult movie fans will find hundreds of reviews on the most varied films. In the section "About the blog", its author mentions:

In the section "About the blog", the author mentions: "Generally, modern Hollywood blockbusters will not be commented on; rather, films unknown to the general public, rare or forgotten, with an emphasis on those shot in the sixties, seventies and eighties; mostly from Europe (and Asia). Special emphasis will therefore be placed on "cult", alternative, underground, low-budget, "B series", "exploitation" films; of various genres and subgenres: horror, giallo, sword and sorcery, peplum, polizziesco, chanbara/jidaigeki, italo-western, cine quinqui...

Some of these films are of a very high artistic quality and of great plot interest, but either because they were not distributed properly at the time, or because they are not "American" or for any other reason, today they are ignored by the "ordinary citizen" and do not have the recognition they undoubtedly deserve".

For a fistful of dollars (O.V. Per un pugno di dollari)

Italy, 1964

Director: Sergio Leone

Script: Sergio Leone, Jaime Comas, Víctor Andrés Catena, Fernando Di Leo, Duccio Tessari, Tonino Valerii

Cast: Clint Eastwood (Joe), Marianne Koch (Marisol), Gian Maria Volontè (Ramon Rojo), Wolfgang Lukschy (John Baxter)

Music: Ennio Morricone

Plot

A rider arrives at a Mexican border town called San Miguel. As he drinks water from a well, he witnesses a child trying to meet his mother being kicked by an individual. The woman, who sees the stranger arriving, is held up.

The stranger goes to the town's cantina. The innkeeper informs him that the town has become a very violent and dangerous place, as two rival groups of bandits try to control the smuggling business. San Miguel, very close to the US border, is a strategic point through which shipments of weapons and alcohol pass; the bandits sell this merchandise to the Indians. The Rojo family on one side and the Baxters on the other are fighting for hegemony, with the result that the death rates from gunshot wounds are very high there. The old gravedigger, who also builds coffins, has numerous "customers".

The newcomer is looking for work. Upon entering the village, some Baxter thugs shot near the legs of his horse while he was riding, in an attempt to frighten him away. When the outsider learns that the most powerful gang is the Rojo Brothers, he turns to them for a job. To prove his worth, he confronts the Baxter bullies who had previously harassed him. He insists that they apologize, but when they laugh in his face and draw their guns, the outsider quickly eliminates the four of them.

"El Americano" (whose name is Joe, although he is only called that once) is hired by the Rojo brothers, Benito and Esteban. The most fearsome of the three brothers, the bloodthirsty Ramón, is not there at the time. Soon a convoy of Mexican soldiers will pass through the town, and the Rojo brothers ask Joe to keep an eye on them. The stranger overhears a conversation between the two brothers: Esteban protests that Miguel has given him too much money, and thinks that it is not necessary to support him. So "el Americano" prefers to go and live in the cantina run by Silvanito.

The stranger sees the woman who was being held at the entrance of the town again at the Rojo's house. When he asks the bartender who she is, he learns that she is Marisol, with whom Ramón is completely in love. "The best thing is to forget about her". Joe, accompanied by Silvanito, decides to go out to the shores of the Río Bravo to watch over the military convoy. There they observe hidden behind some dunes the transference that is going to take place between the Mexican and the U.S. soldiers. The Mexicans are carrying a shipment of gold to buy an arsenal of weapons. However, the Americans are betraying the Mexicans, killing them all once they have taken the gold. In reality, the supposed gringos were not such, but Ramón Rojo and several members of his gang (as Silvanito confirms), who had dressed up in Yankee uniforms (for which they had previously killed U.S. soldiers as well). After the massacre, they place all the bodies in such a way that it seemed that they had killed each other and leave with the gold.

One of the Mexicans gets up, gets on his horse and almost manages to escape, but Ramón shoots him when he has gone far enough away, knocking him down. The stranger is impressed by the bandit's good aim.

Later, Ramón returns to town with his brothers and they introduce him to the new member of the gang, "el Americano". Ramón proposes to make a truce with the Baxters so that there will be peace in the village for the time being. Everyone will have to conduct themselves with discretion to avoid attracting the attention of the authorities after the spectacular coup. It is expected that both the Mexican and U.S. governments will open investigations after the border massacre.

From the first moment, Ramón is suspicious of the outsider his brothers have hired: "He's too smart," he says. And indeed, the Americano sets in motion his plan to pit the two rival gangs against each other and take advantage of the discord: With Silvanito's help he takes two bodies of the fallen soldiers in Río Bravo to the cemetery and places them there next to a grave with rifles in their hands as if they were alive and lying in wait. After that, he returns to the town and warns Ramón that two of the soldiers managed to escape and are now barricaded in the cemetery... At the same time, the stranger enters the Baxters' house and tells them that the Reds have committed the carnage of the border to get the gold. In this way he intends to lure them to the cemetery outside San Miguel as well. While the gunmen from both gangs are there, distracted and shooting at each other, Joe has a clear path to get into the warehouse where they are hiding the stolen gold. After knocking out the guard, the outsider looks for the loot in the barrels. When he finds it, he's surprised by somebody approaching. Thinking he is the watchman who has come to his senses, the Americano punches the him. But it turns out to be Marisol, Ramón's lover. The stranger takes her outside; it's too late for the gold as the Rojo´s men are returning. Joe takes Marisol to the Baxters' house, so they can take care of her until she recovers.

So, the Rojo brothers think Marisol has been kidnapped by the Baxters, and they take one of the rival family hostage as well. The exchange takes place the next morning, and an emotional scene occurs when Marisol's little son tries to hug her. Marisol is a married woman with one child, but since Ramón has become infatuated with her, she must live separately from her family.

That night, the bandits of the Rojo brothers celebrate a banquet. The stranger pretends to be so drunk that two men must carry him to his room. But once they are gone, Joe gets up easily and goes out the window, for he wants to settle a matter that very night: he goes to the house where Marisol is being held, liquidates the guards who are keeping her there, and releases her. The woman is finally able to meet her husband and son. The stranger gives them some money and urges them to leave as soon as possible and to cross the border, before the Rojo people arrive.

Obviously, the Americano wants to give the impression that those who rescued Marisol were the Baxters. So he leaves signs of struggle in the house, overturning tables and shelves as if a fight had taken place between many men.

The stranger returns to his lodging... But lying in his bed, Ramón awaits him, he has discovered his trick. The Americano, whose dangerous double game has been thwarted, is sadistically beaten by the Rojo henchmen, who try to make him talk so that he will reveal Marisol's whereabouts. Ramón and his people torture him for hours and leave him half dead, locked in a cellar.

But when it definitely seems that the stranger's shot backfired, he still manages to escape, and begins to prepare his revenge: The final encounter with the heartless Ramón, who like him is an expert with firearms...

Commentary

This excellent Italian-Amerian western was the first masterpiece made by the brilliant (though not very prolific) Sergio Leone. Until then, the Roman director had only released a few minor peplums ("The Last Days of Pompeii" in 1959 or "The Colossus of Rhodes" in 1961). With "For a Fistful of Dollars", the previously unknown Clint Eastwood also rose to stardom.

So great would be the success of this film that in the following years Leone would shoot two more films of the genre (also with Eastwood as protagonist): "For a few dollars more" (1965) and "The Good, the Ugly and the Bad" (1966). Clint Eastwood creates with his imposing presence a character for the whole trilogy: the enigmatic "Man with no name"; a not very talkative stranger, with a hieratic expression, lonesome, cunning, a great marksman; always wearing a poncho, a hat and a little cigar at the corner of his mouth.

The evil Ramón Rojo (brilliantly played by Gian Maria Volontè), is a merciless villain, but his charisma manages to go beyond the screen.

Akira Kurosawa would go so far as to sue Leone on the grounds that "For a handful of dollars" was nothing more than a plagiarism of his 1961 chanbara "Yojimbo" ("The Bodyguard"), whose plot is virtually identical: a ronin who, upon arriving at a village where two rival gangs are competing with each other, tries to make the most of it by offering his services to both of them, pitting them against each other. This was not Kurosawa's original idea either, since the Japanese director had himself been inspired by a classic film noir: "The Glass Key" (Stuart Heisler, 1942).

In my opinion, "For a Fistful of Dollars" is better than its Japanese predecessor. It is more shocking, more brutal, more tense and if that were not enough, there is the sublime music of Ennio Morricone (a fundamental element of the entire Leonian Dollar Trilogy). In this film, the soundtrack (usually without texts) contains, besides the characteristic whistles, whips cracking and an ephemeral voice that seems to repeat something like "we can fight!"

Also the credits, with the silhouettes, are worth mentioning.

Sergio Leone signed the film with the pseudonym "Bob Robertson", in homage to his father (Robertson: son of Roberto). At that time, Italian directors and actors used to adopt English names because they believed that if the film looked foreign, more viewers would come to the cinema.

Sergio Corbucci, also an important director of westerns, claimed to be the first to advise Leone to watch "Yojimbo", the film that inspired him. Fernando Di Leo, another great Italian director, participated with Leone and Corbucci in the writing of the script of "Per un pugno di dollari".

Martin Scorsese, who vindicates and extols the Dollar Trilogy, considers Leone a renewer of the (by then) outdated western genre; Leone was a filmmaker who revitalized the genre with new and powerful archetypes.

For a few dollars more (O.V. Per qualche dollaro in più)

Italy, 1965

Director: Sergio Leone

Script: Sergio Leone, Luciano Vincenzoni, Fernando Di Leo, Fulvio Morsella

Cast: Clint Eastwood (Monco), Lee Van Cleef (Colonel Douglas Mortimer), Gian Maria Volontè (The Indian), Mara Krupp (Mary), Luigi Pistilli (Groggy), Klaus Kinski (John Wild)

Music: Ennio Morricone

Story

A somber-looking bounty hunter arrives in a New Mexico town called Tucumcari. Near the sheriff's quarters he sees a "wanted" sign for a bandit named Callaway, and he sets out to catch him. In the saloon he finds out his whereabouts. It is not difficult to locate him and after confronting him, he eliminates him without further complications, since he is a very accurate marksman.

After collecting his reward, he finds a new sign and sets out to do a new job. But the sheriff warns him that behind this fugitive there is another bounty hunter, a certain "Monco".

Monco is already in the saloon and has spotted his prey. After beating the criminal to a pulp, his buddies intervene (one of them has rushed out of the barbershop and has only half a shaved face). But Monco, whose handling of the gun is prodigious, finishes off all four of them (including Cavanage, the escaped bandit) in a few seconds.

At the same time, not far from there, a group of Mexican outlaws release their leader, who was in prison. Using dynamite and killing all the prison guards (except one, so he can tell what happened) the fearsome bandit known as "El Indio" escapes from the prison in a spectacular escape.

For his head, a much bigger reward is offered than those of Callaway or Cavanage: $10,000. And the same amount for the members of his gang, a dozen men. The two bounty hunters see the poster with the image of the Indio and both, each in his own way, begin to follow his trail.

The Indio is a cruel and heartless outlaw, a sadistic psychopath. He goes looking for the individual who turned him in to the

19

authorities, now married with a young son. The baby is 18 months old, just the time the Indio spent behind bars... He takes the woman and child outside and has them killed; while he challenges the man to a duel: They will have to draw their respective guns when the music of a pocket watch that the Indio always carries with him stops. As expected, the escaped criminal is faster than his inexperienced opponent.

The more mature bounty hunter, always dressed in black, also has a pocket watch identical to the Indio's. Mortimer, the mournful character's name, decides to leave for El Paso because the most important bank in the whole area is located there and he is sure that the Indio and his gang will try to strike there. Monco, too, heads for El Paso. Both bounty hunters settle in their respective hotels, one in front of the other and very close to the bank, waiting for the outlaws to appear.

The Indio and his men have barricaded themselves in a ruined church near the city. Soon several of the Indio's henchmen arrive in El Paso and start surveilling the bank. For indeed, as Mortimer supposed, they intend to rob it. The Indio has gained access to privileged information that will be useful to him in robbing the bank, since he knows that most of the money is not in the "official" safe, but in a corner of the office in another safe hidden inside an ordinary wooden cabinet.

In the local saloon, Mortimer has a tense encounter with one of the Indio's henchmen. Mortimer provokes him to check his reaction. If he does not respond, it is because he is preparing something big, and thus he will have confirmation that he is a member of the dangerous fugitive's gang.

While the bandits control the bank and its guards, the bounty hunters control them; with binoculars from the windows of their respective hotels. In this way, Monco and Mortimer become aware of each other's presence, thus suspecting that they have a competitor. Mortimer discovers that his intuition was correct by browsing the newspaper library and discovering a photo of the bounty hunter Monco, who, in turn, consults an old man known as "The Prophet", who reveals that the other is a former colonel named Douglas Mortimer.

The two become rivals in this way. One night a challenge takes place between the two, after Monco tried to get his opponent to leave El Paso. But when they realize that in addition to having common goals they are so evenly matched in their firearms expertise, they decide to seal an alliance: capture the Indio and his cronies together and then split the juicy reward. Mortimer proposes that "one act from the outside and the other from the inside", that is, that one of the two infiltrate the gang. That should be Monco's role, as Mortimer is already known from the confrontation that took place in the saloon. To be accepted into the group, Monco will have to free one of the Indio's men who is still in prison.

The Indio usually consumes marijuana, and falls into phases of drowsy and melancholy memories while he contemplates his pocket musical watch, which has a photo of a young woman inside...

In order to avoid the authorities appearing in El Paso at the time of the big heist, the Indio designs a maneuver to mislead: He sends four of his men to make a small hit on a less important neighboring town shortly before. One of those four will be

Monco... This one takes the opportunity to get rid of the three bandits.

While the Indio and the rest of his acolytes successfully carry out the explosive robbery (dynamiting the walls of the bank and taking away the cabinet with the safe), the two bounty hunters plan how to liquidate the whole gang.

Mortimer, for his part, asks his partner to leave the Indio to him. The ex-colonel seems to have a score to settle with the bloodthirsty wrongdoer - a personal matter in which the musical pocket watch is the link...

Commentary

What for me are undoubtedly the two best trilogies in the history of cinema (Coppola's "Godfather" and Leone's "Dollar Trilogy") have mainly one thing in common: The second part is as good as the first or even better. The fact that the sequel matches or surpasses its predecessor is almost never the case, besides the exceptions of "The Godfather II" or "For a few dollars more" (whose title is a typical and obvious indicator that the film is a sequel).

So big was the success of "For a Fistful of Dollars" that the following year Sergio Leone and his team decided to film a new western, in which both Clint Eastwood (in the role of the "hero") and Gian Maria Volonté (again "the bad guy") would participate. Lee Van Cleef or Klaus Kinski were also destined to be part of the cast. The apocryphal western remake of the chanbara "Yojimbo" (Akira Kurosawa, 1961), would thus have a continuation.

This time, however, the two main actors in the first part would play roles that, although similar, were different: For Ramón Rojo, the villain of "For a Fistful of Dollars" had died. Gian Maria Volontè is now another Mexican bandit, also histrionic and unpredictable, equally thirsty for blood and gold. Clint Eastwood's character, on the other hand, is called "Monco" instead of "Joe" this time, but is basically the same. This lone gunman, with his poncho, his hat and his little cigar, has become an icon - and not just in the world of the western genre, but in the cinema in general ("The Man With No Name").

Clint Eastwood, by the way, hated having to constantly carry the little cigar in his mouth during filming (he never smoked it). When Leone hired him in 1965 for the second part, Eastwood asked him to make his character non-smoking this time. But Leone told him that was impossible, because the little cigar "was the real protagonist".

Lee Van Cleef gives life to the mature military man, ex-colonel turned bounty hunter, equally lonely and taciturn man - whose motivation to find the Indio goes beyond dollars... (the personal revenge of the protagonist is a resource that Leone would use again for his last western "Once upon a time in the West" in 1968)

Klaus Kinski has a secondary role as one of the Indio's henchmen. The two scenes in which his character has relevance are extremely memorable: In both he confronts Mortimer and the tension grows up in the atmosphere.

Two other supporting actors repeat in the second part of the trilogy (also with different roles): Mario Brega (the fat, bearded lackey of Ramón Rojo, who is now "el Niño", one of the Indio's henchmen) and Joseph Egger ("The Prophet", who in the previous year's film played the elderly undertaker).

If in "For a Fistful of Dollars" the mysterious lone gunman tries to make a profit by taking on the two gangs that control a small town, in "For a few dollars more" there is only one gang, but two "mysterious lone gunmen" - who are initially rivals but decide to ally themselves.

Once again, the excellent soundtrack is provided by maestro Ennio Morricone. The structure and style of the composition is very similar to the music of the first part, but here more melodies are included based on whistles and also elements like the mouth harp.

Among the most remarkable scenes are the confrontation of the two bounty hunters, with Monco firing again and again at Mortimer's hat on the ground, driving it further and further away and preventing him from picking it up; and how the colonel then "takes revenge" by firing repeatedly at his opponent's hat in the air, without even letting it fall to the ground... Thus they show each other that they are "tied" in terms of gun skills.

And as in all of Leone's westerns, the sequence of the duel, the final confrontation, is sublime in every respect (Morricone's music contributes powerfully to this).

Fernando Di Leo, a great director of polizzieschi such as "Milano Calibro 9" (1972) or "Il Boss" (1973) returns as one of

24

the scriptwriters although he is not accredited. The role of director of photography was played by Massimo Dallamano ("La polizia chiede aiuto", 1974).

Django

Italy, 1966

Director: Sergio Corbucci

Script: Sergio Corbucci, Bruno Corbucci, Fernando Di Leo

Cast: Franco Nero (Django), José Bódalo (General Hugo Rodríguez), Loredana Nusciak (Maria), Eduardo Fajardo (Jackson)

Music: Luis Enriquez Bacalov

Plot

A man walks through the desert dragging a coffin with a rope. It's Django, a veteran of the Northeastern army turned into a lone outlaw. Next to an old wooden bridge he sees how some Mexicans have tied up a woman and are preparing to whip her. Before he can intervene, individuals with red scarves arrive and wipe out the Mexicans. But they are not preparing to release the captive; on the contrary, they now intend to torture her. Django confronts the five of them and with the speed of lightning draws his revolver and kills them.

The woman's name is María, and as we will see later, she is half gringa and half Mexican. That's why both sides try to claim her for themselves. Django and María arrive at a ghost town of muddy streets, which has suffered the consequences of the constant confrontation between the Mexican bandits and the guys in the red hoods and scarves - the latter being American confederate rebels under Major Jackson. Although the civil war has ended, with the victory of the northern unionists, Jackson's group continues to fight. The Mexican bandits, in turn, are rebels against their country's government.

In the semi-abandoned town, Django and María arrive at Nathaniel's posada-saloon, where they find, rather bored by the lack of customers, the chorus girls-prostitutes who are at the service of both Jackson's rebels and the Mexican outlaws. Django continues to drag his coffin, to the amazement of Nathaniel and the girls. Through the innkeeper, we learn the reasons why the town is practically uninhabited, since it is the scene of daily shootings between Jackson's "Reds" and the Mexicans of renegade General Hugo Rodríguez. But all this is something Django already knows in advance. He already knows both of the contending leaders. And he has a personal matter to settle with one of them...

Major Jackson and his red hoods shoot at Mexican prisoners for fun and to practice their marksmanship. When Jackson learns that a mysterious stranger with a coffin and a woman has just arrived in town, he goes to Nathaniel's saloon to meet him. Jackson believes that it is the same man who killed five of his men by the old wooden bridge.

The group of Southern rebels collect "protection" money from Nathaniel's business. This time, besides collecting the money as usual, Jackson also has a great interest in seeing the newly arrived guest. Thus, to the already existing confrontation between the Red Hoods and the Mexican subversives, a new element is added: Django, the lonely coffin gunman...

Commentary

There are many analogies between Western films and Japanese samurai films. In the case of Italian-style westerns (or "spaghetti-westerns") this is more than obvious. Not only in the style, in the plot premises and in the characteristics of the main character and the other characters, but sometimes also in the plot itself. It is common knowledge that Sergio Leone was inspired by the story of Kurosawa's "Yojimbo" (1961) for his first Western: "For a Fistful of Dollars" (1964), the film that would make the then still unknown Clint Eastwood a star. The Japanese filmmaker protested against the apocryphal Italian remake, which he considered a plagiarism - when the truth is that Kurosawa had also "borrowed" for Yojimbo certain ideas from a French film...

The story of a wandering gunman (or a ronin in the case of the chanbara) who arrives in a remote village where there is a confrontation between gangs is already a classic; a recurrent starting point in both Japanese jidaigeki and Italian-America westerns productions. This is also the case in Sergio Corbucci's "Django", which we are reviewing today; one of the most famous and emblematic films of the whole genre together with the "Leonese" Dollar Trilogy.

The lone gunman after whom the film is named is a mysterious individual, who seems to have something very specific in mind, but whose intentions we will gradually come to know as the film

27

progresses. To the town besieged by Jackson's "reds" and the Mexican bandits he does not arrive simply by chance. And inside his coffin he does not exactly carry a corpse, but something very much related to death...

Django places himself in the center of the confrontation. And there, symbolically, is also the female figure María (although not of her own free will); who, let's remember, is half Yankee and half Mexican.

The few businesses left in the ghost town must pay "protection" taxes to Major Jackson (as if he were the Mafia). He and his hooded henchmen are in perpetual conflict with General Hugo's Mexicans. Django will try to take advantage of the situation, but going "smart" ends up bringing him unpleasant consequences - like the "man with no name" in "For a Fistful of Dollars".

Both Jackson's Reds and Hugo's gang are "rebels" who fight against the governments of their respective countries: the US and Mexico. Thus, when Jackson's group is seriously harmed by Django's "weapon of mass destruction," the Southern leader will ally himself with the Mexican soldiers - sworn enemies, in turn, of the defector General Hugo. Django will join the latter in executing a coup (the gunman saved Hugo's life in the past), but when there's a lot of gold at stake, even the most fraternal friendships risk becoming brittle... and even more so in a place as inhospitable as the old, wild west. It is clear, as on so many other occasions, that tactical pragmatism and ephemeral alliances are basic components of any armed conflict.

Just as the character embodied by Trintignant in "Il grande Silenzio" (which Corbucci would shoot a little later) has a weapon that is unusual for the space-time context (a German semi-automatic Mauser gun), our Django also has a very special "little friend" (as Tony Montana would say): It is nothing less than a machine gun.

Just as "For a Fistful of Dollars" would make Clint Eastwood famous, "Django" catapulted Franco Nero, a young actor who was only 24 at the time, to fame - although for the role he was "aged" about a decade by make-up. María is embodied by Loredana Nusciak, an actress who also stood out in the Italian-Western genre (with titles such as Romolo Guerrieri's "10,000 Dollars for a Massacre").

This time the superb soundtrack is not composed by the maestro Morricone (as in Leone's Westerns or Corbucci's next), but by another great of film music: the Argentinian Luis Enríquez Bacalov, who a few years later would create the unforgettable score of "Milano Calibro 9" (1972), a masterful polizziesco by Fernando Di Leo - becoming the composer of this director's headline. By the way: Although he is not accredited, the brilliant Di Leo was one of the scriptwriters both in Leone's films and in this "Django".

Ruggero Deodato, who later became famous with "Cannibal Holocaust Canniba", was assistant director to Corbucci in "Django".

Although after the success of this film dozens of westerns were shot that included the word "Django" in the title, there is only one official sequel: "Django 2: The Return" (Nello Rosatti, 1987), also starring Franco Nero.

A gun for Ringo

Italy, 1965

Director: Duccio Tessari

Script: Duccio Tessari, Alfonso Balcázar, Enzo Del'Aquila, Fernando Di Leo

Cast: Giuliano Gemma (Ringo), Fernando Sancho (Sancho), Lorella De Luca (Miss Ruby), Nieves Navarro (Dolores)

Music: Ennio Morricone

Plot

Shortly before Christmas, the outlaw Ringo, nicknamed Angel Face, is released. He was in prison for the murder of gunman Bill Benson, but it could be established that he acted in self-defence. Benson's four brothers are looking for Ringo to settle the score. Ben, the sheriff of Crystal City, hears about the situation and also tries to find Ringo - but to keep more blood from flowing. However, he arrives too late... The Benson brothers locate "Angel Face" and he easily eliminates them before they can even draw.

The sheriff arrests Ringo, charging him with the new murders. Meanwhile, the Mexican bandit Sancho and his cronies plan to rob the bank in Crystal City with the complicity of the attractive Dolores. The young woman must distract the sheriff while Sancho and the others rob the bank. The Mexicans succeed in their mission and flee to a nearby ranch owned by Major Clyde, who is the father of Ruby, Sheriff Ben's fiancée. Sancho's bandits take the girl and her father hostage, as well as the dozens of farm workers who work on the ranch.

Faced with the dilemma, Bill decides to release the expert gunman Ringo on the condition that he infiltrate the Mexican bandits to rescue Ruby and recover the money. Ringo agrees, provided he is officially acquitted of the Benson brothers' deaths. He also wants 30% of the money stolen by the Mexicans.

At the same time, widowed rancher Clyde tries to court Dolores, the only woman in the gang. Ruby blames her father for this attitude, but he assures that it is only a strategy to allow them to escape. Pedro, Sancho's right-hand man, is attracted to the beautiful Ruby.

Bill and some soldiers stand around the hacienda that the Mexicans have taken over, while they wait for reinforcements to arrive. Meanwhile Ringo introduces himself to Sancho and his men, claiming to be a fugitive who has escaped from Crystal City and requesting to join the gang. Initially Sancho and his henchmen do not trust him, but when Ringo shows them his expertise with the gun they agree to take him into their ranks. In addition, Sancho is wounded by a bullet during a shoot-out in the robbery and when Ringo "operates" him he manages to gain the trust of the bandits' leader.

Still, Sancho and his henchmen are treacherous and plan to kill Ringo when he is no longer useful to them. The animosity between Pedro and Ringo, especially because of Ruby, will complicate things.

The reinforcements Sheriff Bill has requested are slow in coming. Ringo ends up telling the Mexicans that he is an infiltrator in the pay of the sheriff but that he is willing to switch sides if they pay him 40% of the loot. Is Ringo really an unscrupulous mercenary who sells himself to the highest bidder? Or is that maneuver part of his tactic to break up the gang?

Commentary

Very entertaining and enjoyable this Christmas western, one of the first to come out in Italy, a blockbuster and very popular, which would have a sequel that same year. It was released shortly after "For a Fistful of Dollars" (Sergio Leone, 1964) - the emblematic feature film with which the sub-genre was launched, and in which Duccio Tessari, director of the proposal under consideration, served as co-writer.

"A Gun for Ringo" lacks the epic tone that characterizes Leone's western films, and also the melancholy, somber and hypervolent style that is typical of many Italian western gems. The plot is simple and linear, yet rich in nuances and well-crafted characters. The usual vendettas are dispensed with and we are presented with a story of hostage-taking with its corresponding intrigues, albeit in a light-hearted and humorous way. Ringo is very different from the Leonesian/Eastwoodian "man with no name": Although he is also an amoral loner he is much more talkative, and often makes joking remarks. He is well dressed, well shaved, does not smoke and drinks only milk. Just as in the film he is a "turncoat", he also switched sides earlier during the civil war: "At first I was with the Confederates, but when I saw that they were losing, I switched to the North. You should never be with a loser... it's a matter of principle".

The film (shot in Almería) was directed by Duccio Tessari, director of the giallo "The bloodstained butterfly" (1971). Tessari also wrote the script, with the collaboration of Spaniard Alfonso Balcázar.

Ringo is played by the famous Giuliano Gemma, whom we saw in other memorable westerns such as "Long Days of Vengeance" (Florestano Vancini, 1967) and "Day of Anger" (Tonino Valerii, 1967) - in the latter together with Lee Van Cleef. Gemma also participates in "Tenebre" (1982) by Dario Argento.

As his antagonist we have a regular actor of the subgenre, habituated to characterize Mexican bandits: Fernando Sancho, who had similar roles in "10,000 dollari per un massacro" (Romolo Guerrieri, 1967)

The female component of the cast falls to Spain's Nieves Navarro as Dolores and Italy's Lorella De Luca as Ruby. The latter takes part in the aforementioned "The bloodstained butterfly" (1971) by Tessari. Nieves Navarro appears in "Naked violence" (1969) an interesting but unknown thriller by the master Fernando Di Leo; and also in "So sweet, so dead" (Roberto Bianchi Montero, 1972).

Once again, Ennio Morricone's masterful soundtrack is worth mentioning.

Massacre time (O.V. Le colt cantarono la morte e fu... tempo di massacro)

Italy, 1966

Director: Lucio Fulci

Script: Fernando Di Leo

Cast: Franco Nero (Tom), George Hilton (Jeff), Linda Sini (Brady)

Music: Coriolano "Lallo" Gori

Plot

Tom is a gold digger in New Mexico. One day he receives an unexpected visit from an old acquaintance from his hometown. The man brings him a brief note: "You must return." Many years ago, after the death of his parents, Tom left his village. His brother Jeffrey is the only relative he still has there. The messenger does not know who is sending him the letter or why. Intrigued, Tom decides to leave his companions who are looking for gold nuggets in the rivers to return to the village.

Once there, Tom searches for his brother but no one seems to know him. His family's ranch now has other owners, the Scott family. Mr. Scott and his fearsome son Junior have taken almost complete control of the town, and they also own the bank and the saloon. Scott's anagram, a crossed T and S, can be seen in most stores and homes. A Chinese man who seems to work as a blacksmith tells Tom where to find his brother.

Jeffrey, who has become an alcoholic, lives with the old Mexican maid Mercedes in a cabin outside. Before meeting them, Tom gets to witness the arrival of Scott and his henchmen in town and witnesses Junior's savage cruelty to the locals - who are exploited and extorted by the gang.

As soon as he sees Tom, drunkard Jeffrey asks him when he plans to leave. It is not he, then, who has sent him the message begging him to come. Jeffrey and Mercedes think it's best for Tom to leave as soon as possible, for his own good. They seem to know something they're trying to keep from him. But the gold digger, once back, wants to find out who made him come. Tom also observes with growing indignation the arrogance of the Scott family and their thugs, who have taken over his family's ranch.

That night, in the local saloon (where the Chinese man previously seen works as a pianist), a fight breaks out between Jeffrey, Tom and Scott's henchmen. The brawl is about to escalate from fists to guns, but strangely enough, what appears to be the chief of Scott's hit men (an Indian) orders his cronies to stop. Tom realizes that they could have been killed perfectly, or tried to be killed at any time, but for some reason he does not understand why they chose not to. This is particularly odd considering the way these individuals who dare to challenge them spend their time - something Tom had seen firsthand that morning.

Meanwhile, at the Scott ranch, Junior senses that his father is trying to remove him from managing his property. The young man has an unpredictable and overly aggressive personality, impossible to control. The father tries to stop him from causing trouble, and the disenchanted Junior begins to realize it...

Tom decides to go to his old friend Carradine's house to explain the mystery surrounding Scott and his gang. But the thugs have followed him from the saloon, and before Carradine can reveal anything, he's murdered. They also ruthlessly execute his wife and two daughters. But, once again, they don't try to kill Tom...

Jeffrey, who knows where the Scott ranch is, finally agrees to accompany his brother - seeing that it is impossible to convince him to leave. To get there, both of them will have to overcome numerous obstacles...

Commentary

A remarkable western by Lucio Fulci, with an original and solid plot and the characteristic style of the best films of the genre at the time.

The question that Tom tries to solve on his return is related to his past, to his origins... Tom and Jeffrey are brothers, but, as will be seen in the second half, only on their mother's side. Jeffrey's father was killed by Scott... And who is Tom's real father? The obvious answer to this question can be seen coming before the middle of the film.

The Scott's have set up a reign of terror in the village and have an army of ruthless gunmen. But old Scott's relationship with his son Junior is not the best. The father is a plunderer and a leech, but the son is more than that, he is a bloodthirsty psychopath. That's why the father called his first son (who is none other than

Tom); so that he would be his right hand and heir... How will Tom react to this unexpected discovery? We will not reveal it, but it goes without saying that the evil Junior will not stand idly by...

This is one of the two westerns directed by Lucio Fulci, the other being "I quattro del Apocalisse", filmed in 1975, when the genre had already gone out of fashion. The protagonist of this "Time of Massacre" is Franco Nero, the actor who played the successful original "Django" by Sergio Corbucci (also in 1966). Fulci, who would later be known as "The Godfather of Gore", already gave a glimpse of his predilection for showing scenes of explicit violence. The film opens with a prologue in which we see a man being chased by angry dogs, which the Scott family have unleashed against him. The unfortunate man is caught in a pond by the beasts, which tear him to pieces; the water turns red... The sequence of the duel between Tom and Junior, as well as the final assault on the Scott house, is extremely memorable.

The character of the multi-employed Chinese adds a comic note. This hard-working Asian is a blacksmith, pianist, undertaker... whatever it takes. He also handles confidential data and is an informer - only in exchange for money, of course. And, like a good Chinese, he always has a proper Confucian proverb handy.

The script was written by the great Fernando Di Leo - who later became the director of masterpieces such as "Milano Calibro 9" (1972) or "Il Boss" (1973). Di Leo also collaborated with Sergio Leone in the writing of "Por un puñado de dólares" (1964), a legendary western shot in Almería that would make Clint Eastwood famous.

I will highlight a couple of curiosities: The alcoholic Jeffrey (played by the Uruguayan George Hilton) proves to be an exceptional shot with a gun despite his love of drinking. He is also very polite: Shortly before shooting his opponents, he calls them saying "Excuse me, gentlemen...".

When the brothers arrive at the Scott ranch, they have a party and everyone there, both men and women, are dressed completely in white - a color that paradoxically symbolizes purity and innocence. "You have done so much for the progress of this land..." one woman says raptly to old Scott, who has really done nothing but usurp that land and enslave its true owners. The hypocrisy and cynicism of the powerful are thus portrayed.

The soundtrack was composed by Lallo Gori (author of the music of "The Wolf Woman"), and includes a song in English as the main theme that reminds in its style to that of another recommendable Italo-Western, "Mannaja" (Sergio Martino, 1977).

The good, the bad and the ugly (O.V. Il buono, il brutto e il cattivo)

Italy, 1966

Director: Sergio Leone

Script: Sergio Leone, Luciano Vincenzoni

Cast: Clint Eastwood (the Blonde), Eli Wallach (Tuco), Lee Van Cleef ("the Bad"), Rada Rassimov (Maria)

Music: Ennio Morricone

Plot

Tuco ("the Ugly") is an outlaw wanted for a long list of crimes, who always manages to evade the authorities.

At the same time, a sinister gunman arrives at a family's home for the purpose of getting important information. The woman and son leave, and the newcomer intimidates the man while he is eating. The man suspects that the individual is a thug sent by Becker, who sends him to find out the whereabouts of a box full of dollars from a robbery. The gunman wants to know where a man named Jackson is, and what name he is using now. Well, "if he hadn't changed his name, I'd have found him long ago."

The father ends up confessing that Jackson is now calling himself "Bill Carson". The hit man says Becker paid him $500 to kill him. The man gives him $1000 to leave him alone, but the gunman replies that when someone pays him he always does his job... and shoots him dead. He also kills the son, who appears moments later with a shotgun, after which he takes the $1,000.

The murderer returns to Becker (an old, sick man in bed), and informs him that he has completed his mission. He also informs him that the man he has just killed paid $1,000 to eliminate him, Becker... and as "when someone pays me I always do my job" he also kills him, with several shots in the face. This ferocious gunman ("The Bad"), with 1500 dollars, now sets out to find Jackson (aka Bill Carson) and especially the box of money that he supposedly hides.

Meanwhile, Tuco is approached by three armed men who try to capture him. A rider in a trench coat appears and easily eliminates them from three accurate shots. But the blond gunman had not acted this way to protect the bandit, but to hunt him down himself, thus collecting the reward. The Blond ("the Good") takes Tuco to the sheriff while the sheriff insults and curses him.

Tuco is going to be hanged. He already has the rope around his neck and the executioner reads before the executioners the long litany of crimes of which he is accused. But the Blond, standing on top of a nearby barn, shoots the rope and rescues the outlaw. The two escape from the village on horseback. Both share the money (which increases after each new escape of the bandit) and as partners they repeatedly carry out the same strategy: The bounty hunter delivers and releases Tuco again and again (in different villages), always collecting the reward for the same criminal (with whom he shares it).

"The Bad" continues the search for Bill Carson, and in one of the towns he passes through finds Tuco about to be hanged. But he immediately detects the trick that he and his "blonde guardian angel" are pulling. When he finds out that Carson was seen in a neighboring town called Santa Ana with a certain Mary, the shady gunman heads there.

After one of his escapes, the Blond decides to dissolve the partnership with Tuco and abandons him in the desert, taking all the reward. After a long wander through the arid sands, the bandit reaches a village where he can finally drink water, and get hold of a gun in a gun shop - which he mugs with the gun he was supposed to buy.

The hitman in black interrogates Mary in Santa Ana about Bill Carson's whereabouts. These are the years of the American Civil War, between Northern Yankees and Southern Confederates. According to the girl, Bill has left for Santa Fe as a soldier in a South American company. He's lost an eye and now wears a patch instead.

Tuco is willing to make him pay for his betrayal of his ex-partner. After locating the hotel he's staying at, he catches him coming in through the window (while the Blond is busy shooting at gunmen stationed at the door). Tuco forces him to stand on a stool with his neck stuck in a gallows hanging from one of the ceiling beams. "I won't shoot at the rope, but at one of the stool's legs..." However, outside, a fierce gun battle is taking place between the Yankee and Southern troops. Fortune smiles on Rubio when one of the cannon balls hits the building where the two are standing, sinking the ground and freeing himself. The stunned Tuco observes that his prey has escaped.

41

For his part, "the Bad" reaches what is left of the Confederate military camp, reduced to a few smoking embers. Inquiring about Bill Carson, he is informed by one of the soldiers that he was taken prisoner by the Nordists, who took him to a concentration camp.

Tuco tirelessly continues the search for the Rubio, and tracks him through the desert collecting cigarette butts from his cigars. When he finally finds him, the bounty hunter was about to shoot at the rope of another condemned man, a certain Shorty, with whom he had entered into a new "partnership" like the one he had with Tuco in the past. The Blond is disarmed by his opponent, who prevents him from shooting at the rope and thus saving Shorty's life.

Now Tuco has a free hand to implement his cruel revenge: His intention is abandon the Blond to a slow death in the torrid desert sands, a long agony under the relentless sun. Thus begins a long march through the desert: Tuco on the back of his horse, with hat, umbrella and water bottle; having sadistic fun while the Blond must walk exhausted and thirsty until he collapses...

When Tuco is about to finish off Rubio it seems that once again good luck is on the side of "Good": A horse-drawn carriage is approaching from the horizon. It is a Southist military detachment, but inside there are only corpses left. Tuco greedily plunders them. He notices that one of them is still alive: He is a badly wounded recruit with an eye patch. The soldier tells him to give him water, and in return he will reveal the whereabouts of a treasure: $200,000. The dying man is none other than Bill Carson. He says the money is hidden in a cemetery coffin, but he is unable to pronounce the name of the grave in which the dollars are hidden. Tuco runs to get the canteen, and when he returns he sees that the Blond has crawled to Carson, who has already expired. But before he dies, the soldier has given the name of the grave to the Blond.

Now they need each other again and have no choice but to become partners again: For one knows the name of the cemetery and the other the name of the grave. They both put on their Southern uniforms, and Tuco pretends to be "Bill Carson" (putting on his eye patch as well). The Mexican bandit who until recently was trying to bring his companion to an agonizing and suffering death now wants to save his life at all costs. Tuco takes Rubio to the infirmary of a convent, and there the bounty hunter recovers little by little. The superior friar, Pablo Ramírez, is Tuco's brother. The two fight: Tuco asks about his parents, and the friar answers with bitterness "only now do you remember them. It's been nine years..." Both their parents are dead. The friar accuses Tuco of having chosen the wrong path and he replies: "If one does not want to starve in the world from which we come, one has only two options: Become a friar or a bandit. You have chosen the first and I have chosen the second, which is the harder of the two"...

Once they leave the convent, when the Rubio is fit again, both are arrested by a detachment of Northern soldiers. Tuco and his companion were still wearing Confederate uniforms. When Tuco saw the soldiers approaching, whose uniforms looked gray from afar, he cheered them on. But as they got closer it turned out that they were blue (Nordists) who were returning covered with dust from a battle and therefore seemed to be wearing grey jackets like those in the south...

Tuco and the Blonde end up in a Yankee prison camp. The commander is dying of gangrene, and it is the second in command who gives the orders: This is Sergeant "Sentence"... none other than the gunman in black (i.e. "the Bad") who was looking everywhere for Carson to get to the treasure through him.

Sentecia, who has seen Tuco and Rubio among the prisoners, is willing to get the information from them to get to the $200,000; under torture if necessary...

Commentary

The third part of the Dollar Trilogy is also the longest and most ambitious, as well as generally the best rated by critics. If "For a Fistful of Dollars" (1964) had only one protagonist (Stranger Joe) and "For a few dollars more" (1965) had two (The Bounty Hunters "Monco" and Mortimer), "The Good, the Ugly and the Bad" (1966) has three: The Trio of Gunmen already mentioned in the title.

Clint Eastwood's phlegmatic character (this time called "The Blond") is slightly different from his equivalent in previous installments, especially in terms of aesthetics: In the last film of the Eastwood trilogy he no longer wears his famous poncho, but a trench coat. But the little cigar continues to be worn on his lips (Leone already said that this little Tuscan cigar "was the real protagonist"; and this time its relevance is greater, since Tuco was able to follow the Blond's itinerary and reach him by picking up his cigar butts in the desert).

Only in the final scenes, from the passage through the North American military camp and after the bridge is blown up, does Eastwood put on his characteristic poncho again; which seems to be exactly the same as in the other two films. The colt that Clint wears in "For a Fistful of Dollars" and "For afew dollars more" has a picture of a coiled snake on the butt. In "The Good, the Ugly and the Bad" his gun seems to be a different revolver, with a much longer barrel.

Originally, Leone had foreseen that the role of the "Bad" would fall on Henry Fonda, an actor very much appreciated by him. However, he ended up playing him as Lee Van Cleef, who had already collaborated in "For a few dollars more" as Colonel Mortimer. Henry Fonda would be the antagonist of the archetypal "lone gunman" in the epic "Once upon a time in America" (1968), the last western by the Roman director.

The respective plots of the films that make up the Dollar Trilogy have no connection whatsoever with each other (as is the case, however, in the Godfather Trilogy). What unites them (apart from their genre and period) is their visual and narrative style, their plot outlines and the presence of the main actors themselves (especially Clint Eastwood). And also, as is obvious, having been conceived by the same director, the same team of scriptwriters and having all three with colossal soundtracks by the master Morricone.

The new face in the third installment is that of "Ugly", the tongue-in-cheek, buffoonish Mexican bandit Tuco (full name: "Tuco Benedicto Pacífico Juan María Ramírez"). Played by Eli Wallach, Tuco's character adds a nice note of humor and irony - By the way, just as Eli Wallach appears in the third part of the

Dollar Trilogy, he also plays an important role in the third part of the other fundamental trilogy; that of the Godfather. In "The Godfather III" (1990), an elderly Wallach characterizes Mafia boss Osvaldo Altobello.

These three implacable men are condemned to collaborate to reach the treasure. The three hate each other, but at the same time they need each other. "The Good One" is indeed the least bad of the three, and the only one who really deserves his nickname (although an even more suitable nickname would be "the Wily One" - for not only his marksmanship but also his intelligence is more than proven). The other two are completely unscrupulous, and plan to stab their opponents in the back at the first opportunity (after having found the dollars, of course).

"The Good, the Ugly and the Bad" is a western with light comedic touches (mostly black humor) framed in the context of the American Civil War. The main characters have the opportunity to witness fierce fighting between the two sides, the Yankee Unionists in the North and the Confederate Secessionists in the South.

The film contains (in part because of its almost 3-hour length) more remarkable scenes and great dialogue than its two predecessors in the trilogy. Among them is the one about Tuco's robbery at the armory; or the one about the one-armed man who bursts into the room where Tuco is in the bathtub with the intention of settling his score: The one-armed man thinks he's surprised, points a gun at him and starts lecturing him that he'll make him pay dearly for his misdeeds. Tuco, who has the pistol hidden under the foam of his bathtub, simply shoots him and utters a laconic and lapidary phrase: "When you shoot, you shoot, you don't talk".

It's very funny the enormous cynicism of Tuco, who in the monastery's infirmary tells the friars to "take good care of my friend, he's like a brother to me" - when a few hours earlier he was walking the Blond through the desert to slowly kill him with thirst and exhaustion (of course that was before he knew about the existence of the cemetery's treasure). The Blond, on the other hand, says a highly memorable (and paradoxical) phrase while he is convalescing in the infirmary: "I will sleep peacefully because I know that my worst enemy is watching over me" (No one can hurt him if even his worst enemy tries to protect him).

The scene of the triple duel in the central square of the cemetery is one of the highest peaks of Leone's cinema and one of the best western sequences of all time. Three greats, Clint Eastwood, Lee Van Cleef and Eli Wallach; ready to draw and pull the trigger. Close ups to their restless eyes, sweaty foreheads and alert hands. All of this is spiced up by the chords of Morricone's excellent soundtrack...

As a curiosity: 1500 Spanish soldiers participated as extras in the film (shot in Almeria). Lee Van Cleef had the middle finger of his right hand partially amputated, which can be seen if you pay attention during the dueling scene.

Another legendary phrase (and one of the last ones in the film) is the one said by the Blond to Tuco in the cemetery: "The world is divided into two categories: Those with loaded guns and those who dig..."

Django kill! (O.V. Se sei vivo spara!)

Italy, 1967

Director: Giulio Questi

Script: Giulio Questi, Franco Arcalli

Cast: Tomás Milian (Stranger), Marilú Tolo (Lori), Piero Lulli (Oaks)

Music: Ivan Vandor

A masterpiece of "spaghetti-western" (a genre which, by the way, has always been infinitely more interesting to me than Western cinema shot in the USA), on a par with Sergio Martino's "Mannaja" and, in my opinion, far superior to Corbucci's "Djangos" and this director's "Grande Silenzio". In its filmic field, only the movies by commercial Leone manage to surpass it.

Giulio Questi, for me a complete unknown, offers us more than 100 minutes of pure visual enjoyment full of surprises, proposing forceful slaps to the conventions of the genre. Because the film we're dealing with here is far from being a "spaghetti" with an ordinary plot. This brilliant film, condemned to ostracism by both film experts and film lovers, has rightly been described as a "surrealist gothic western" and has even been compared to "El Topo", a jodorowskyan contribution to the Seventh Art that appeared a couple of years later.

The first thing we see is a hand coming out sinisterly from the desert sands. It is the hand of the protagonist, whose name is never mentioned throughout the film and who is called "the stranger". The actor who brings him to life is a very convincing Tomas Milian, an ideal performer for the role and who participated in many Spanish-Italian products of the time. Some Indians who prowled around those contours discover the dying man and manage to heal him. All they want in return is for him to tell them what the world of the dead is like, since he has returned from the beyond. The Indians have turned the gold dust that the Stranger had in his pockets into bullets, so that he can take revenge on those who had left him in such a pitiful state; half-dead and buried.

To get to know the background of the starting point I have just narrated, we see in a lysergic flashback sequence that Tomas Milian, the nameless "stranger", belonged to a gang of multicultural outlaws who took over a huge shipment of gold by robbing the retinue of soldiers who were transporting it. The problems came during the cast: The group is composed of American "WASP", Mexican Indians and our hybrid protagonist, considered "mestizo". The former, captained by a scoundrel nicknamed "The Oak," are not willing to share the fruits of their mugging with these "dirty Indians," so they are ruthlessly liquidated by shooting them with laughter.

Up to this point, the viewer thinks: "Of course, now the Stranger will look for the traitors to take revenge; that is the plot of the film. (But he's wrong...)

For their part, the gringo bandits arrive in a poor, unhealthy and oppressive village, where they must acquire new horses to continue their journey with the stolen gold shipment.
The villagers, primitive and shady degenerate beings who radiate an atavistic animality, have discovered that they are bandits and brutally lynch them (to get hold of the gold, there is no other reason, even if they cynically appeal to justice and order).

They are massacred with ferocious sadism and hanged in the square amidst shouts of joy (hilarious is the scene where one of the bandits has his cigar taken out of his mouth to put the rope around his neck and then put it back in).

Only one has managed to escape from the municipal fury and bloodlust: The Oak, the boss, the most important one.

At that moment we see a recovered Tomas Milian arrive in the village, who is preparing, cold and undaunted, to take revenge on The Oak; which, surrounded by the villagers, stands in a store shooting from the window. The Oak, with extreme terror, believes that the stranger is a ghost. So he spits at him: "If you're alive, shoot!" (hence the original title of the film). And he sure as hell shoots: It leaves him like a sieve, although it doesn't kill him. To all this, there is a cacique rancher in the arid town, who covets gold, escorted by his "boys" (a detachment of rough gunmen dressed in rigorously black, who, as will later become more noticeable, establish an aesthetic reminiscence with the contemporary "urban tribe" of homosexual sadomasochistic leather bikers).

The fat rancher insists on leaving the Oak alive so that he can confess under torture the place where the golden treasure is hidden. They take him to the saloon to extract the bullets, and there the mob of villagers discover that the bullets are not made of lead, but of gold. They rush at the dying man like hungry hyenas to voraciously extract the particles of the precious metal, discarding him and causing his death, to the disappointment of the chieftain and his acolytes.

What they don't know is that the gold has previously been put into safekeeping by two individuals: The owner of the saloon and Hagerman, another powerful figure in the municipality who keeps his sister cloistered in a room because in his opinion "she is crazy". The outsider Milian, who observes the ghostly female from the sandy village square, feels a strong attraction to her from the beginning, as he sees her leaning out of the window.

The two gold holders compete with each other and will try to take each other's share. In retaliation and as a form of blackmail, the rancher orders the kidnapping of the saloon owner's son, a teenage boy to whom the disturbing "boys" give more than lustful looks. Milian intends to free him, and the rancher who is holding him throws him a challenge: The kidnapped boy is hanging from the ceiling by the hands of a rope, the outsider must cut that rope with one shot, placing himself ten paces away from the young slope. But in addition to this test of skill, Milian has to drink half a bottle of whisky before he can take up the challenge: "I want to see if you're not only a good gunman, but also a good drinker," says the sly chieftain.

So far I have told you, and no more, about the plot and subplots of this convoluted and surprisingly atypical western; full of

51

metaphysical, allegorical (Tomas Milian resembles a mystical figure on more than one occasion - he was even crucified), satirical and surreal elements.

A timeless cult film, a fusion between Almeria spaghetti and Gothic terror, with lysergic and hallucinogenic touches (which in fact makes it a precursor to "El Topo").

Special mention to the animalistic cast: The alcoholic parrot and the bomb-horse.

The long days of revenge (O.V. I lunghi giorni della vendetta)

Italy, 1967

Director: Florestano Vancini

Script: Fernando Di Leo, Augusto Caminito (based on the story of Mahnahén Velasco)

Performers: Giuliano Gemma (Ted Burnett), Francisco Rabal (Sheriff Douglas), Gabriela Giorgelli (Dulcie), Nieves Navarro (Dolly)

Music: Armando Trovajoli, Ennio Morricone

Plot

Ted Burnett, convicted of the murder of Colonel Steiger, manages to escape from prison after three years of hard labour.

Mr. Cobb, a cacique from an area bordering Mexico, is a cruel and unscrupulous individual. He leads a gang that terrorizes the region and is involved in arms trafficking, which he supplies to a Mexican rebel general. When Cobb learns of the prisoner's escape, a great uneasiness takes hold of him. And he is not alone in fearing Burnett's revenge: His partners Sheriff Douglas and Judge Kincaine are also on high alert.

For Burnett was sentenced to 30 years in prison when he was innocent. His father, who owned a railroad company that he should have inherited, was liquidated and his possessions passed to Cobb and his associates. As if that wasn't enough, Ted's fiancée was kept by Douglas.

Cobb and Douglas' men immediately set out to find the fugitive. They rightly sense that Burnett, instead of crossing the border to hide in Mexico, will go on the offensive against them.

After eliminating some gunmen who were on his trail, Ted arrives at the home of Gómez, Cobb and Douglas's lieutenant. Burnett wants to know who killed his father, so he can confirm his suspicions about the conspiracy to take over the railroad company.

Later, in another village, Ted saves a quaint hawker and wandering charlatan nicknamed "Little Bird" from being lynched by the locals. The latter is busy touring the villages with his niece Dulcie, selling useless knick-knacks and pretending to be a doctor. In exchange for his help, Ted asks Little Bird to transport him hidden in his caravan to Card Town, the place where his enemies are.

Once there, Ted Burnett will seek to settle the score with the three criminal usurpers responsible for his imprisonment and the death of his father: Chief Cobb, Sheriff Douglas and Judge Kincaine .

Commentary

The film we are reviewing today is a western adaptation of "The Count of Monte Cristo". The screenwriters are the great Fernando Di Leo (who later would make his own films, specializing in the gangster-police genre) and the lesser-known Augusto Caminito, an identical tandem of authors who the following year would write "The Ruthless Four" (Giorgio Capitani, 1968).

The protagonist's girlfriend, who after her imprisonment became the "property" of the corrupt sheriff Douglas, is faced with an emotional dilemma when Burnett reappears: While on the one hand she is happy to see him again, on the other she has been married to Douglas for three years now, she feels protected and "indebted" to him - a kind of Stockholm syndrome. This will complicate things, as well as Ted's growing attraction to Dulcie, the travelling salesman's niece.

Giuliano Gemma, whom we have already seen in another memorable western, "Day of Anger" (Tonini Valerii, 1967), embodies this "Count of Monte Cristo" from the wild west called Ted Burnett. At first he is unrecognizable with his long hair and beards, as well as his dirty, tattered clothes. That appearance contrasts sharply with his elegant white suit and the dandy look that he displays later on.

The film, although quite routine in its execution, has some surprises towards the final stretch; as well as scenes worth mentioning. Among them is the tense sequence of Burnett being shaved by Gómez. The knife in the hands of the conspiratorial trio's lackey barber is too much of a temptation. But Burnett, who holds his revolver under the towel, doesn't lose sight of Gómez' hand for a second as he is shaving him. Burnett's trick with the thread in his match against Douglas is also very original, as is the sheriff's penchant for practicing his aim by throwing his service star, as if it were a ninja shuriken.

Douglas is played by Paco Rabal, who in those years took part in many Italian productions - among them "Il Consigliori" (Alberto de Martino, 1973), a sort of rip-off of "The Godfather" (Francis Ford Coppola, 1972).

The director Florestano Vancini (who signs under the pseudonym of "Stan Vance") would later film the second installment of the mini-series saga "La Piovra" (in 1986).

The soundtrack, composed by Armando Trovajoli, has the uncredited collaboration of the master Morricone.

$ 10,000 Blood Money (O.V. 10.000 dollari per un massacro)

Italy, 1967

Director: Romolo Guerrieri

Script: Franco Fogagnolo

Cast: Gianni Garko (Django), Loredana Nusciak (Mijanou), Adriana Ambesi (Dolores)

Music: Nora Orlandi

Plot

Django is a bounty hunter in the wild west. He makes his living as a lone gunman by catching or killing the escaped criminals who are on the classic "Wanted" posters. One of them is the recently released Mexican thug Manuel Vásquez.

In one of the first scenes of the film, Django and Manuel cross paths on horseback in the desert without knowing who the other one is, exchanging suspicious glances. Soon after, Django (who was on his way to a town to deliver the body of a criminal) sees a sign in the sheriff's office asking for $3,000 for Manuel's head, which he has just stumbled upon on the way...

Manuel and his cronies head to the hacienda of the wealthy Señor Mendoza, with whom they have a score to settle. Once there they provoke a massacre, shooting at the landowner's workers, leaving only the landowner alive. Manuel had it in for Mendoza because he sent him to jail. Mendoza cowardly begs

Manuel to spare his life, and crawls like a worm, begging for mercy. The criminal fugitive has come to take something, but it is not money or precious metals. It's not dollars but Dolores that Manuel wants; Mendoza's beautiful daughter. The criminal and his people are taking the girl hostage.

Mendoza has heard about Django's skill with colt and decides to hire the gunman to rescue his daughter. The landowner promises the bounty hunter $5,000 for the abductor's head, $2,000 more than what was listed on the sign.

In the village hall, an attractive young woman of French origin named Mijanou works as a waitress. She is a friend, a sort of girlfriend, of Django, who has a peculiar love-hate relationship. Mijanou hates the profession of the lonely gunman, and warns him hostilely about it; but deep down she is in love with him.

Manuel is a very well-known individual in that locality, he frequently plays cards in the saloon and does not hesitate to settle without contemplation those who dare to cheat. Django keeps a close eye on him, waiting for the right moment to cut him down. Manuel senses that the bounty hunter will try to catch him, and tries to get ahead of him: they ambush him and shoot him from a hill. Django falls from his mount, badly wounded, and Manuel's men assume he is dead. But Django, who has been shot in the shoulder, manages to get up and with the help of the photographer (who was passing by in his horse-drawn carriage) returns to the village, where he receives Mijanou's attention.
When the next morning the gunman feels better, his friend tells him that she is fed up with the dusty village, the constant gunfights and her work as a bounty hunter, and that she is

57

considering going to San Francisco. Django answers that he is willing to leave everything and go with her. Mijanou, excited, accepts and the two kiss passionately.

But a few moments later, Mendoza arrives, accompanied by the photographer (who will now become Django's "squire"). The landowner, who wants to see his daughter Dolores free at any cost, doubles the reward: he now offers $10,000 for Manuel's head. Django accepts, but only if he pays in advance and Mendoza does so. Mijanou is furious and feels betrayed, but finally agrees to wait six days for Django to fulfill his last bounty hunting assignment. If after that time Django hasn't returned, she'll go to San Francisco alone and won't want to see him again.

So Django (who has already collected the money) gets "down to business", and finds out about Manuel's whereabouts by interrogating one of his henchmen. The fugitive is in another village, hidden in his father's house. The gunman arrives there to confront Manuel. But when he finally locates him, instead of killing him he agrees to rob a stagecoach caravan carrying a load of gold bars as partners...

Commentary

"10,000 dollari per un massacro" is a conventional Italo-Western, but with the particularity that it has several unpredictable twists in the plot, and that it is marked by tragedy... For among the carriages that Django and Manuel blow up during the execution of their robbery is one aboard which is Mijanou, the girlfriend of the protagonist. She dies as a result of the explosions caused by Django himself, which deeply affects him. As if that weren't enough, the crawling Manuel flees, taking all the gold with him, without sharing it with his "partner" who helped him strike. After that, Django will now make every effort to hunt down the bandit.

During the sixties, many films were shot in Italy, starring a taciturn gunman named "Django". The best known is the original, by Sergio Corbucci ("Django", 1966); with Franco Nero giving life to the character. Then came the "Ringo", the "Sartana"... But the most famous of all these lonely bounty hunters who perform feats with the gun is precisely one who has no name: The "Man with no name" (sometimes called "The Blond") from Sergio Leone's Dollar Trilogy, a role that launched Clint Eastwood into stardom.

This Django was played by Croatian-born actor Gianni Garko.

Playing Dolores we have Adriana Ambesi, who we already saw in "Malenka" (1969) by Amando de Ossorio, as a vampire. Although Dolores' character is key to the development of the story, the girl in only appears in very few scenes and hardly says a word.

Manuel is played by none other than Claudio Camaso, whose real name was Claudio Volonté, brother of the great Gian Maria ("El Indio" from "For a few dollars more"), to whom he certainly looks quite similar. The personal story of the actor who plays the bandit Manuel is also quite intricate: accused of murder, Claudio Camaso ended up in prison, and there he committed suicide in 1977.

The soundtrack of "10.000 dollari per un massacro" is quite good, but it doesn't reach the level of the ones composed by the brilliant Morricone for the Leone Westerns.

Requiescant

Italy, 1967

Director: Carlo Lizzani

Script: Adriano Bolzoni, Armando Crispino, Lucio Battistrada, Pier Paolo Pasolini, Carlo Lizzani (Based on the story by Renato Izzo and Franco Bucceri)

Cast: Lou Castel (Requiescant), Mark Damon (George Bellow Ferguson), Pier Paolo Pasolini (Don Juan), Barbara Frey (Princy), Franco Citti (Burt), Ninetto Davoli (El Niño), Mirella Maravidi (Edith Ferguson)

Music: Riz Ortolani

Plot

A truce is about to be sealed in a border area between the United States and Mexico. But when the agreements have been reached, the gringos begin to treacherously shoot on the Mexicans. Men, women and children perish under the bullets. The massacre has been ordered by landowner Ferguson.

Not far from there rides a lone rider known as "Requiescant". He is a Mexican, adopted son of a priest, who has received a very religious upbringing and is never separated from his Bible in

60

Latin. During his travels he has been forced to wield his gun against various enemies, discovering that he has an almost supernatural talent for handling a revolver.

The young Princy, also the priest's adopted daughter and therefore a kind of sister to Requiescant, has allegedly left her family to go with a caravan of comedians. Requiescant is determined to find her, find out what really happened and bring her back.

At the nearest town hall, Requiescant discovers that Princy is being held against her will and exploited as a prostitute. He tries to convince her to escape, and assures her of his protection. But the girl insists that this would be too dangerous, for the saloon belongs to the powerful Ferguson, lord and master of those lands.

Requiescant decides to go to Ferguson's estate to talk to him personally. Posing as a priest, he seeks to persuade him to release the girl. Ferguson pretends to accept, but first Requiescant must show his providential skill with the revolver in a dangerous game: Both will compete by shooting at the candlesticks held by Edith, the rancher's wife. They will have to take turns extinguishing them with bullets - each time from a greater distance and drinking a glass of wine between shots.

Actually, Ferguson has no intention of letting Princy go. Least of all Dean Light, Ferguson's lieutenant who personally controls the saloon prostitution business. To him, Princy is his "goose that lays the golden eggs." So they ambush Requiescant, but miraculously he manages to survive: the Bible he keeps in his jacket pocket protects him, preventing the bullet from reaching his heart.

Requiescant releases Princy and both leave the village where the girl was held, while Ferguson's henchmen are on their heels. An old mute helps them by providing shelter. The mute tries to make Requiescant understand that years ago there was a brutal massacre there and nearby (the same one we saw in the initial scene). Requiescant finds the skeletons of dozens of people, including children, discovering that Ferguson is a much more evil individual than he had imagined...

Commentary

A curious western that mixes religious and class struggle themes (which has certain analogies to liberation theology) with the characteristic style of the subgenre: Revenge, enigmatic lone gunman and exacerbated violence. The film manages to captivate from the very first moment, with the raw sequence of the carnage in which the Mexican peasants perish. Requiescant is a figure of mystical proportions that reminds us of the second part of Alejandro Jodorowsky's "El Topo" (1970). It also bears a striking resemblance to the Zatoichi saga, for like the blind masseur brought to life by Shintaro Katsu, this Requiescant is forced to kill enemies against his will (always in self-defense), and repents (praying for them) every time he eliminates somebody.

The scene of the shooting competition between Ferguson and Requiescant is particularly tense and memorable. It also highlights something that Ferguson himself will later explicitly admit: That his wife's life is of no importance to him (Edith holds the candlesticks that they try to blow out with shots, and the more steps she takes the more risk she runs of being hit by bullets).

The film features a minor role for the famous director Pier Paolo Pasolini - who also collaborated in writing the script, although without being credited. There are also two typically Pasolinian actors: Ninetto Davoli and Franco Citti, the latter as a sadistic gunman. Ferguson is characterized by Mark Damon, whom we saw in "Byleth (il demone del incesto)" (Leopoldo Savona, 1972) or in "Nude... si muore" (Antonio Margheriti, 1968).

Ferguson's contempt for women and his ambiguous relationship with his lieutenant suggest certain homosexual inclinations on the part of the sadistic villain.

"Requiescant" was directed by Carlo Lizzani, director of the truculent giallo "Storie di vita e di malavita" (1975), which also deals with prostitution.

The soundtrack is by Riz Ortolani, whose best known music is that which accompanies the footage of "Cannibal Holocaust" (Ruggero Deodato, 1980).

Da uomo a uomo (a.k.a. Death rides a horse)

Italy, 1967

Director: Giulio Petroni

Script: Luciano Vincenzoni

Cast: Lee Van Cleef (Ryan), John Phillip Law (Bill), Mario Brega (Walcott's Henchman), Luigi Pistilli (Walcott)

Music: Ennio Morricone

Plot

Outlaws with faces hidden by scarves attack a village on a stormy night. They break into a family's home: father, mother, teenage daughter and young son. As the man prepares to grab his shotgun, he is riddled with bullets. The four bandits then pounce on the women to rape them. The boy has been able to hide in time and looks on in terror. Shortly afterwards, his mother and sister are also killed. Before they run away, the boy gets to see some characteristics of the attackers that will remain engraved in his memory: One of them has a deck of cards tattooed on his chest. Another wears an eye-catching earring. They set fire to the house, and the boy is about to be burned to death. But someone wearing a skull pendant saves him from perishing in the flames.

Once outside, as he watches his house burn with tears, little Bill finds a spur in the sand. It undoubtedly belongs to one of the raiders...

Fifteen years later, Bill is a young man who has acquired great mastery of the gun. He trains his marksmanship daily, hoping to get revenge on his family's killers. However, so far he has no leads. All he has left is the spur he picked up and the terrible memories of that night.

At the same time, not far from there, the mature Ryan is released after spending fifteen years behind bars. The prison warden gives him back the $80 and the gun that were confiscated at the time of his arrest. With part of the money he buys a horse at the prison gates. Once outside, he notices two riders following him. For the moment he manages to throw them off.

Ryan arrives in a town, the same one in which is Bill, and he's staying there in a hotel. Young Bill is struck by the presence of the stranger. The sheriff of the village, who was a friend of his father's, proposes Bill to work for him as a deputy. But the boy is not interested in stable employment, he just wants to find his family's killers as soon as possible.

That night, two gunmen sneak into the hotel room where Ryan is staying. They are the two horsemen who have been following him since his release from prison. Ryan was waiting for them, and he takes out the gunmen before they open fire. These are definitely hit men. The sheriff acknowledges that Ryan acted in self-defence, but urges him to leave the village. As he examines the bodies, the sheriff notices one detail: The spurs worn by the hit men are identical to those Bill picked up that tragic night 15 years earlier...

The sheriff informs Bill about that. Thus, the young man discovers that there is a connection between the mysterious stranger and the murderers in his family. They both seem to have the same enemies. Bill follows Ryan and proposes an alliance. But Ryan rejects it, as he finds the young man too impulsive.

Still, Bill follows the veteran gunman to the next town. He's sure he knows who those four bandits were and will lead him to them.

Like Bill, Ryan also has a score to settle with those four. They're responsible for him spending 15 years in prison. Now, these four outlaws, his former accomplices, are rich, powerful, "respectable" men. One of them was the one who sent the hit men to wait for him when he got out of prison. Ryan wants to collect $15,000 from each of them, as "compensation". 1,000 for every year spent behind bars. The former bandits, now turned bankers or big business owners, are each in a different village but are still connected. When one of them dies after being challenged in a duel by an enigmatic young man, the other three begin to worry and take action.

That will force Ryan, who is separately seeking revenge, to join "impulsive" Bill. The paths of the two will then cross again...

Commentary

"Da uomo a uomo" is a story of parallel vendettas that end up converging. Two men, one young and one in his sixties, seek to settle the scores of four former outlaws who have climbed the social ladder to become part of the upper class. The motives of both are quite different. And when the circumstances push them to collaborate, they begin to realize that they were already in front of each other fifteen years before... Where was Ryan that fateful night?

In this exciting and highly recommended western we have the star presence of Lee Van Cleef, well known for appearing as a hieratic bounty hunter in two of the feature films that make up Sergio Leone's Dollar Trilogy: "For a few dollars more" (1965) and "The Good, the Bad and the Ugly" (1966).

A familiar face for Italian-Western fans is also Mario Brega, who here plays the head of Walcott's Mexican thugs (one of the outlaws who fifteen years later is a banker). Brega appears in supporting roles in the aforementioned Leone films, as well as in "For a fistful of dollars" (1964) and "Once upon a time in America" (1984).

Luigi Pistilli, who gives life to Walcott, was also seen in films by Leone and in "Il grande Silenzio" (Sergio Corbucci, 1968); usually in villain roles. He also appears in "Milano Calibro 9" (Fernando Di Leo, 1972) or "Gli assassini sono i nostri ospiti" ("Killers are our guests") (Vincenzo Rigo, 1974).

Burt Cavanaugh, another of the former outlaws (recycled into "respectable citizens") is played by the Scottish Anthony Dawson. The same name would be used as a pseudonym by the director Antonio Margheriti.

The soundtrack is composed by Ennio Morricone, a regular musician for the "spaghetti-westerns" and other Italian films of the time.

Day of Anger (O.V. "I giorni dell'ira")

Italy, 1967

Director: Tonino Valerii

Script: Ernesto Gastaldi, Tonino Valerii, Renzo Genta (based on a novel by Rolf Becker)

Cast: Lee Van Cleef (Frank Talby), Giuliano Gemma (Scott Mary), Christa Linder (Gwen), Al Mulock (Wild Jack), Álvaro de Luna (Wild Jack's henchman)

Music: Riz Ortolani

Plot

Young Scott performs the most humble tasks in the village of Clifton. He's a garbage man, a sweeper, a cleaner of toilets and stables. The villagers despise him and consider him an outcast. This is mainly due to his family background: He is the son of a single mother and it is not known who his father was. Judge Cutcher insults him by calling him a "bastard", and prevents him from getting close to his daughter. The owner of the saloon is also one of the people who most viciously vilify the boy. In a stable Scott keeps an old gun and trains himself to handle it.

One day, a mysterious stranger arrives in Clifton, just passing through. He asks Scott where he can stay and promises him a dollar in exchange for taking care of his horse while he stays in town.

When Scott goes to the saloon to collect his dollar, the owner tries to throw him out; his presence is not welcome there. But the stranger, named Frank Talby, wants the boy to stay, since he is his guest. Perkins, another customer of the establishment, insists on throwing the "bastard" out. Inevitably a confrontation between Perkins and Talby takes place: The former sets out to draw his revolver, but Talby is quicker and kills him. At the trial, Judge Cutcher is forced to acquit Talby; he acted in self-defense and there are witnesses to corroborate this.

Shortly thereafter, Talby leaves Clifton and continues on his way. Perkins was a powerful man in the area, and Scott knows that his men will soon come for revenge. And not finding the stranger would make them angry with him - for he was the source of the saloon clash. Scott decides to leave the village and follow Talby, to put himself under his protection. The young man sees the mature gunman as a potential master.

So, when Scott reaches Talby, he offers himself as his disciple and assistant. The lonely rider is sceptical at first, but soon begins to give Scott his particular "lessons", realizing that the boy learns quickly.

Talby, followed by Scott, arrives at an arid village near the Mexican border. In the cantina he searches for a certain Wild Jack. He is an outlaw with whom he has been associated in the past and with whom he has a score to settle...

They were both involved in a train robbery ten years ago. Talby never got his cut, $50,000. Wild Jack says he doesn't have the money either and that he spent all that time behind bars. He claims the loot was divided up by certain citizens of Clifton - hearing his people mentioned gets Scott's attention.

Banker Turner, Judge Cutcher and the owner of the saloon, among others, conspire to get the money from the robbery. Talby prepares to return to Clifton, but Wild Jack tries to sell him out. Talby counterattacks and eliminates his opponent.

Later on, some Mexican bandits, Wild Jack's henchmen, capture Talby and start torturing him, tying him to a horse and making the horse gallop at full speed so that he is dragged through the torrid sands. However, Scott intervenes in time, throwing his master a colt to defend himself. When Talby eliminates the Mexicans with the help of the young man, he realizes the great potential Scott has. He buys him a gun and officially becomes his preceptor.

The two return to Clifton, where Perkins' henchmen soon arrive. Now Scott will have the opportunity to show that he is a real man, and not just a poor, unworthy "bastard".

Both Talby and Scott, master and disciple, share enemies: The banker, the judge, the saloon owner... Clifton's corrupt powers. One considers them enemies for money: They were the ones who kept the loot that Talby stole "by the sweat of his brow". And Scott, for his part, has something personal against these three; for they subjected him to outrageous treatment, a lifetime of humiliation.

Commentary

The same year as the release of "Death rides a horse" (Giulio Petroni, 1967), another western with a similar theme and starring Lee Van Cleef came to the big screen. On this occasion the central theme is also the effort of a young man seeking to acquire the knowledge and practice of a veteran gunman. Scott is an outcast, a true "untouchable" of the old west, the lowest rung on the social ladder. But he has a strong will to excel and is determined to prove to everyone that he is good for more than just picking up trash and cleaning out barns. He is good at using a gun and is not willing to tolerate anyone calling him a bastard anymore.

In this regard, among the memorable moments in the film is the dialogue between one of Clifton's residents and Talby in the saloon when he and his disciple have returned to town: "What have you done with him? (referring to Scott) Now he looks like a rabid wolf". Talby replies, "A wolf is a wolf by birth. *You* have made him rabid".

Scott intends to make his enemies pay dearly for their affronts. Clifton's powerful men who mocked him so much are actually much more despicable than he is: they are hypocrites as well as corrupt. Also in "Death rides a horse" the antagonists were "respectable personalities" - with a dark past as bandits and murderers. Both the plot and the structure are very similar in "Day of anger" and in Giulio Petroni's film.

Moreover, this film by Tonino Valerii is also the classic story of the outstanding student who ends up surpassing his teacher.

Towards the second half, a conflict between Scott and his mentor begins to emerge...

Talby's lessons will be very useful to the young man: Especially "Don't trust anyone" and "If you ever shoot a man, kill him; because if not, sooner or later he will kill you"...

Scott is played by Giuliano Gemma, whom we saw in "Corleone" (Pasquale Squitieri, 1978) and "Tenebre" (Dario Argento, 1982), among other titles. The charismatic Lee Van Cleef plays Frank Talby - a character identical to those the American actor embodies in films such as "For a few dollars more" (1965) or "The Good, the Bad and the Ugly" (1966), both by Sergio Leone.

The feature film we are dealing with, an Italian-German co-production, was shot in Almería; like so many other spaghetti-westerns of those years. The soundtrack was composed by Riz Ortolani, who also took care of the music for "Cannibal Holocaust" (Ruggero Deodato, 1980) and the first installment of the "La Piovra" saga (Damiano Damiani, 1984).

The Bounty Killer (O.V. "El precio de un hombre")

Spain / Italy, 1967

Director: Eugenio Martín

Script: Eugenio Martín, Don Prindle, José G. Maesso

Cast: Tomás Milian (José Gómez), Richard Wyler (Luke Chilson), Halina Zalewska (Eden)

Music: Stelvio Cipriani

Plot

Mexican bandit José Gómez, a fugitive from justice, arrives in a town in the middle of the desert whose few inhabitants help him to hide. The fugitive is followed closely by bounty hunter Luke Chilson.

José hides in a small boarding house run by his girlfriend Eden and her uncle. Soon after, Chilson arrives there to refuel, initially ignoring that the man he is chasing is also there.

The bounty hunter realizes that the bandit is hiding there. José tries to escape, but after a brief gunfight he is reduced and arrested. The authorities want him alive, so Chilson hands him over to the sheriff of the nearest town and charges the $3,000 they offered for his head.

Later, handcuffed Jose Gómez is taken to prison in a horse-drawn carriage, escorted by a detachment of guards. He is apparently a dangerous criminal. The entourage stops for lunch at a tavern where José's friend Eden happens to be.

The two pretend not to know each other so as not to arouse the suspicions of the guards, and in a moment of carelessness, Eden passes a gun to the prisoner under the table. Then the girl leaves, and shortly after that the figures of a pair of horsemen appear on the horizon: they are José's men. They are José's men. A shooting begins between them and the guards, and José takes advantage of this to use the gun he received from his friend to kill the agents who were taking him to prison. Thus, the bandit manages to escape once again.

Again Luke Chilson enters the action, and goes to the town that gave shelter to José Gómez, imagining that he will return there. Chilson is sure that Eden is the accomplice who passed the gun to the prisoner at the inn to make him escape.

Eden tells the bounty hunter that José is a good man and to stop chasing him: He is a bandit who only steals from the rich and helps his people. But Chilson is not so sure about that; he claims he is an unscrupulous killer.

José does return, and two of his men are killed by the bounty hunter. Once again, Chilson manages to disarm José and prepares to hand him over to the authorities again... but everyone in the village supports the fugitive and is ready to defend him with all their might: the villagers now confront Chilson directly, knocking him out when he had beaten the bandit to a pulp.

Once he has recovered, José is about to murder his unconscious opponent in cold blood, finishing him off with a heavy iron on the head, but Eden's intercession prevents him from consummating such baseness. The bruised and bloody Luke Chilson is tied to a pole in the haystack; Joseph and his men plan to have fun torturing him.

The truth is that something in Joseph has changed... Eden and the other villagers are slowly beginning to notice something strange in his behavior. He is no longer an affable and generous "robin hood" as when the villagers met him, now he has become cold and calculating, he is not the same as before; he has become the heartless leader of a criminal gang.

Eden begins to wonder if Luke Chilson might not be right after all...

Commentary

The story and the moral approach of this, all in all, "business as usual ibero-western film, is quite interesting ("business as usual" except for the last ten minutes; with a superb climax). Neither the cold and hardened bounty hunter seeks to capture fugitives only out of greed nor the pursued fugitive is as innocent and a victim of (in)justice as he seemed to be.

"The Bounty Hunter" is one of the many films of the genre shot in Almeria, as an Italian-Spanish co-production. The director of the proposal is Eugenio Martín, director of about thirty films among which is "Horror Express" (1972) with Christopher Lee. Eugenio Martín used the Anglo pseudonym "Gene Martin" internationally.

The Mexican bandit José Gómez is played by Tomas Milian, a Cuban actor living in Italy who took part in many polizzieschi (both serious and humorous) and who is famous in Italy above all for knowing how to imitate very well the ways of speaking and acting used in the Roman underworld. Milian has also worked on other westerns, such as Giulio Questi's "Django Kill!", also from 1967. In "The Bounty Hunter" Milian's character, who at first may be sympathetic, seems to become increasingly alienated as the plot progresses, even acquiring psychopathic traits.

In contrast, the taciturn and icy Luke Chilson (in whose skin the British Richard Wyler gets into) does not change throughout the film; he is constantly the prototypical "tough guy". Eden is played by Polish actress Halina Zalewska.

The (very good) soundtrack is by Stelvio Cipriani, who has composed for Mario Bava, Umberto Lenzi and Joe D'Amato. Unfortunately the quality of the image and sound is very poor in the copies that exist today, to the point that sometimes it is difficult to understand some dialogues.

Quella sporca storia nel West (a.k.a. "Johnny Hamlet")

Italy, 1968

Director: Enzo G. Castellari

Script: Sergio Corbucci, Tito Carpi, Francesco Scardamaglia, Enzo G. Castellari, Bruno Corbucci (based on a play by William Shakespeare)

Cast: Andrea Giordana (Johnny Hamilton), Gilbert Roland (Horace), Horst Frank (Claude Hamilton), Françoise Prévost (Gertry Hamilton), Stefania Careddu (Betty), Manuel Serrano (Santana), Gabriella Boccardo (Emily / Ophelia)

Music: Francesco De Masi

Plot

After the end of the American Civil War, Private Johnny returns to his native Texas. He takes the road back with a traveling company of theater artists. He cannot sleep soundly because of nightmares in which he sees his late father, whose strange death was not cleared up. After saving the artists from the attack of some bandits, Johnny separates from them and arrives at a cemetery excavated inside a cave. There he finds his father's grave, and on the cross the epitaph confirms the young man's suspicions: his father was "vilely killed". To Johnny this had already been revealed in his dreams.

The newly returned war veteran is approached by two thugs, Ross and Guild. But he receives help from Horace, a friend of his father's. When the quarrelsome duo retreats, Johnny asks Horace who killed his father, for he intends to avenge him. What is believed in the village is that he was killed by Santana, a Mexican bandit. But Horace adds that Santana is also dead, since he was already killed by Claude, Johnny's uncle, his father's brother.

When Johnny arrives at the hacienda owned by his family, he discovers that his mother has remarried... to his uncle Claude. Claude now owns the land that belonged to his father. Johnny begins to suspect that Santana's story is a sham, and that it was actually his uncle Claude who killed his own brother to get the family land. Ross and Guild, the thugs who attacked him at the cemetery, are henchmen in Claude's service.

Johnny is reunited with Emily, his old girlfriend. The girl's father, a corrupt man involved in several crimes, is now the town sheriff. The sheriff forbids his daughter to meet with Johnny. And he senses that Emily knows more about her father's death than she's willing to admit. Johnny will try to shed light on the circumstances of the murder. Although he suspects his uncle of masterminding and the involvement of several others, he has no way of proving it. Horace, who assumes a fatherly role towards the young soldier, will try to help him.

Horace shows his protégé the amulet that was found on his father's body, a sort of "signature" of the murderer - supposedly the bandit Santana. It's an ornament with an Aztec relief.

The same theater company that Johnny returned to Texas with arrives in town. Johnny is thus reunited with one of the actresses, a girl who was already attracted to him. In a moment of intimacy, Johnny notices the girl's earrings: They are identical to the Aztec amulet that Santana used to wear to mark his crimes. Johnny begins to think that Santana is still alive, and the doubts he had about the identity of his father's killer only increase.

Soon after, the actress is killed. Someone seemed to want to keep her from talking too much. Some Mexican gunmen try to eliminate Johnny, but Horace intervenes again; saving him.

While Johnny rides off to Mexico to find out if Santana faked his death, his old girlfriend Emily, the daughter of the new sheriff, is also killed. The perpetrator of this new crime leaves the gun marked with Johnny's initials next to the girl's body, so that suspicion falls on him...

At the same time, Johnny's mother begins to realize that her old brother-in-law and new husband kept many things from her about Johnny's father's death...

Commentary

The opening scene, when one of the actors recites a passage from Hamlet, has great symbolic power, as this western turns out to be an apocryphal sui generis adaptation of Shakespeare's famous play. The plot can be described as the classic revenge so typical of Italian-style western, spiced up with touches of classic tragedy and its tangled family conflicts. The film also has some "thriller" in it (although without the aesthetics and stylistic characteristics of the giallo), because of the "investigation" Johnny undertakes to find the murderer (or murderers) of his father (and other new victims).

This is one of the first films in Enzo G. Castellari's long career as a director. A little gem of a western earlier and much less known than the famous "Keoma" (1976).

The initial dream sequence is memorable, as is the gloomy setting of the candlelit cemetery/cave (which is more than likely an allegorical representation of the underworld). As later in "Keoma" the protagonist has to go through the "initiation test" of being crucified (more symbolism with metaphysical transcendence), which he will overcome before embarking on the final stretch of his mission (the ancient archetype of the "resurrection of the hero"). On the other hand, the conflict between the two brothers (Johnny's father and Uncle Claude) is also quite metaphorical, considering the context: The fratricidal American civil war.

Brothers Sergio and Bruno Corbucci collaborated with Castellari in writing the script. Two years earlier, Sergio Corbucci had directed "Django" (1966), and that same 1968 he would shoot "The Great Silence".

We saw Gilbert Roland, who plays Horace, in "The Gold Professionals" (Giorgio Capitani, 1968).

Throughout the film there are many arid and rocky places. The filming took place in the Almería desert of Tabernas, as well as in the Huelva Mining Basin.

Francesco De Masi's soundtrack is out of the "Morriconian school" (whistles, mouth harps, etc) and combines songs in the hippy style or 1960s progressive rock (as in the westerns

"Django", "Keoma" or Sergio Martino's "Mannaja") with solemn choral and organ music (thus emphasizing an almost mystical character of the protagonist).

Requiem for the gringo

Italy, 1968

Directors: Eugenio Martín, José Luis Merino

Script: Enrico Colombo, Giuliana Garavaglia, Arrigo Colombo, María del Carmen Martínez Román
Performers: Lang Jeffries (Ross Logan), Femi Benussi (Alma), Fernando Sancho (Porfirio Carranza)

Music: Angelo Francesco Lavagnino

Plot

Mexican bandit Porfirio Carranza takes over the Ramírez family's ranch on the U.S.-Mexico border. To do so, he has the help of a trio of gringo criminals: The elegant Tom, the "Indian" Charly and the sombre Ted, always dressed in black. However, it is a tense and unstable alliance. The three Americans and Carranza have been forced to collaborate by circumstances, but they hate and fear each other; they are just waiting for the right moment to eliminate each other.

The Ramírez's pawns must now work for the bandits who have taken over the hacienda. Among them is the young Alma. Ted wants her for himself, though she tries to resist him. One day the evildoers find a boy sniffing around. He was talking to Alma, and she seems to know him well. The boy is questioned but refuses to talk. He is tortured by whipping and Ted ends up killing him in a bumpy duel that serves as a show for the whole gang. Horrified, Alma sets out to escape.

Carranza's girlfriend is Nina, who only agrees to be with him in exchange for jewelry and money. In reality, Nina has a relationship with Tom, one of Carranza's "allies". The two conspire to get rid of the bandit chief and seize the treasures he has amassed during his criminal career.

Meanwhile, a mysterious gunman dressed in a leopard poncho approaches these lands. He seems to be an expert in astrology, since according to his calculations something very important is about to happen on April 17, 1867. There are only three days left until that date. The gunman, named Ross, arrives at a boarding house and asks about the Ramírez ranch. He knows that its rightful owners have been expelled and that now some bloodthirsty bandits have settled there. At the boarding house he meets Alma, and when he senses that she has fled the ranch, he asks her for details. Ross has a score to settle with these gunmen, and the day to settle it, according to the stars, is the very near 17th of April.

When Carranza sees the horses of several of his men arrive with their bodies on the saddles, he understands that someone is trying to challenge him. The mysterious rider in a leopard poncho is getting closer and closer to the ranch, while the alliance between the three gringos and the leader of the band is about to break down...

Commentary

This Italian-Spanish co-production can't be accused of being an unoriginal western. Its protagonist is an enigmatic gunman with paranormal faculties and knowledge of astrology, who wears a leopard poncho. The mood is sometimes disturbing, with storms and a dark and oppressive atmosphere contributing to this, as well as scenes of a rather graphic sadistic hypervolence - you can see, for example, how a knife sticks a hand of one of the bandits into the wall, and when he falls the hand is cut in two from bottom to top. The sequence of the lashes is also filmed carefully in detail, reminiscent of a similar situation in Lucio Fulci's "Time of the Massacre" (1966).

The details of the motivation that drives the protagonist towards his confrontation with the bandits are slowly being revealed. The plot is partly based on Masaki Kobayashi's "Harakiri", which serves once again to highlight the undeniable parallels between Japanese chanbara (or "samurai" films) and westerns, especially Italian and European ones - Remember that the story of Sergio Leone's "For a Fistful of Dollars" (1964) is inspired by Kurosawa's "Yojimbo" (1961).

The film was directed by Eugenio Martín, director of the interesting thrillers "Hypnosis" (1962) and "Aquella casa en las afueras" ("That House on the Outskirts") (1980), as well as the western "The Bounty Killer" (1966) with Tomas Milian in the main role. José Luis Merino, a Spanish filmmaker usually more dedicated to horror, collaborated in the direction. The main scriptwriter Arrigo Colombo was one of the producers of the successful film that started the subgenre: The aforementioned "For a Fistful of Dollars" by Leone. Giuliana Garavaglia also collaborated in the writing of the screenplay, and she also participates as an actress playing the role of Lupe - the innkeeper who tries to seduce the protagonist. The latter is played by the American Lang Jeffries, who in Italy is known for his presence in peplums and spy films.

Other characteristic actors of the Italian-Western that we can see in the proposal are Aldo Sambrell (as Charly), Fernando Sancho (as the chief of the bandits) or Marisa Paredes (as Nina). Alma is embodied by Femi Benussi, who we saw in the gialli "Nudes for the Killer" (Andrea Bianchi, 1975) or in "The Killer is Obliged to Kill Again" (Lugi Cozzi, 1975), among other titles.

The disturbing gunman in black is played by Carlo Gaddi, who bears a fairly reasonable resemblance to his compatriots and professional colleagues Franco Citti and Franco Garofalo.

Corri uomo corri (Run, man, run)

Italy, 1968

Director: Sergio Sollima

Script: Sergio Sollima, Pompeo De Angelis

Cast: Tomas Milian (Manuel "Cuchillo" Sánchez), Donald O'Brien (Nathaniel Cassidy), Linda Vera (Penny Bannington), Noé Murayama (Pablo), Orso Maria Guerrini (Raúl), Chelo Alonso (Dolores), José Torres (Ramírez)

Music: Bruno Nicolai, Ennio Morricone

Plot

These are the turbulent years of the Mexican revolution against Porfirio Díaz. The little thief Manuel Sánchez aka "Cuchillo" returns to his town, where he meets his fiancée Dolores. With the intention of giving his girlfriend a gift, he steals a gold watch from a gringo who sleeps nearby. But the gringo notices the theft: It's former sheriff Nathaniel Cassidy, who now resides between Mexico and the United States. Cassidy gets his watch back. Later he and Cuchillo meet again in a tavern. There the thief witnesses the mastery in the use of firearms of the former sheriff, who defeats one who had challenged him in a duel. Cuchillo had bet on him, and so he prevents one of his opponent's cronies from shooting Cassidy in treason.

As he leaves the tavern, Cuchillo is arrested by the police, who see him running around in a suspicious manner. For the commissioner, he is an old acquaintance. The veteran Porfirian police officer knows why the thief is nicknamed Cuchillo: He has at least five bladed weapons camouflaged in his clothes and shoes - and he is an expert at using them.

The detainee is taken to a dungeon where he shares a cell with another individual. This is the poet Rodríguez, an opponent of the regime who has benefited from an amnesty and plans to be released the next day. However, Rodríguez is convinced that this is a trap. That is why he asks Cuchillo to help him escape that very night. If he does, he will pay him $100 once the two of them arrive in Texas.

Meanwhile, outside the barracks where they are both imprisoned, some disturbing men are lurking. Among them, former sheriff Cassidy. Also two French gunmen: Michel and Jean-Paul. They worked first for Emperor Maximilian and then for Porfirio Díaz. Both they and Cassidy are waiting anxiously for Rodríguez to get out of jail, because they know that the poet is hiding an important secret that could make them very rich...

Thanks to a ruse by Cuchillo, Rodríguez and the thief manage to escape that same night. As they left the barracks they met Dolores, who had come to free her fiancé. But to the woman's great disappointment, Cuchillo does not stay with her but goes to Texas with the poet. The humble thief is still unaware that there is more at stake than the $100 that Rodríguez has promised him.

The two arrive at the revolutionary man of letters' village, where he is revered by the locals. But soon some Mexican bandits appear who want to take away the secret of his treasure from

Rodríguez by force: The poet knows where $3 million that belonged to Benito Juárez's movement are. Rodríguez does not want that money for his personal gain, but for the people; to help finance the overthrow of the "porfiriato". The bandits, on the other hand, are of a different opinion, and they want the millions for themselves. They begin to arbitrarily shoot at Rodríguez's countrymen, and when he gets in the way he is also hit by one of the bullets. Then the French gunmen and the former sheriff, who had been following Cuchillo and the poet since their escape, intervene.

There is a chaotic shoot-out between the three newcomers and the bandits. Cuchillo approaches the dying Rodríguez, and before he dies he has time to hand him a piece of paper containing the treasure map. The millions are hidden around Burton City. "Run, man, run..." are the poet's last words. Cuchillo immediately sets off on his way there. He knows Cassidy and the French will be following him. But they're not the only ones: His girlfriend Dolores is also looking for him.

Across the desert, Cuchillo watches as a woman buries a corpse. She introduces herself as Sergeant Penny Bannington, and the dead man is her assistant. The young woman is a very special "sergeant": She belongs to a kind of religious charity called the "Liberation Army". Cuchillo helps the girl to bury the deceased, and when she tells him that she is going to Burton City the Mexican offers himself as her new assistant.

Meanwhile, the French on one side and the ex-sheriff on the other know that Cuchillo knows the secret of the treasure and they are on his tail. For different reasons, Dolores follows him, who will not be happy to find her fiancé in female company...

Commentary

"Corri uomo corri" has as its central theme the search for a treasure by different individuals and factions, which will inevitably lead to numerous entanglements and misunderstandings. The film could be described as a revolutionary and humorous western. It is an Italian-French co-production shot in Almería.

Besides Leone and Corbucci, another Sergio also stood out in the subgenre of the Italian-style westerns: Sergio Sollima. This director had filmed in 1966 "The Big Gundown" (original version "La resa dei conti", which literally translates as "The Settling of Scores"). In that film, the character of funny Mexican bandit Cuchillo, played by Tomas Milian, appears for the first time. The film we are dealing with today can be considered a sequel to the above-mentioned film, although the respective plots are completely independent. Both films have the Mexican revolution as a background. This "Run man run" stands out above all for its use of a certain comedy, brought about above all by the protagonist (with his outbursts, his blunders, etc.).

The temperamental Dolores is played by Chelo Alonso, considered "the queen of the peplum" for having participated a decade before (at the end of the '50s and beginning of the '60s) in numerous epic productions of "sword and sandals". We saw her in "Il terrore dei barbari" (Carlo Campogalliani, 1959) with Steve Reeves; or also in "Atlas against the cyclops" (Antonio Leonviola, 1961) in the company of Gordon Mitchell. Chelo Alonso, a Cuban native like Tomas Milian (and born like him in 1933) also has a small role at the beginning of "The Good, the

Bad and the Ugly" (Sergio Leone, 1966). That and her characterization as the dominant Dolores are her only interpretative contributions to Western cinema.

Former sheriff Cassidy is played by a hieratic and undaunted Donald O'Brien, perfect for the character. We saw the Irish actor in the memorable westerns "The Four of the Apocalypse" (Lucio Fulci, 1975) "Keoma" (Enzo G. Castellari, 1976), and "Mannaja" (Sergio Martino, 1977).

In minor roles we find Orso Maria Guerrini (who appears in "Keoma" and "La Piovra"), and the Mexican-Japanese Noé Murayama ("El Látigo contra Satan") as the revolutionary Pablo.

The soundtrack was composed by Ennio Morricone, but it was signed by his collaborator Bruno Nicolai; since the great master was embarking on another project at the same time (to which he was "officially" to devote himself exclusively).

The great Silence (Il grande Silenzio)

Italy, 1968

Director: Sergio Corbucci

Script: Sergio Corbucci, Mario Amendola, Bruno Corbucci, Vittoriano Petrilli (Dialogues of the English version: John Davis Hart, Lewis E. Ciannelli)

Cast: Jean-Louis Trintignant (Silence), Klaus Kinski (Madman), Frank Wolff (Sheriff Gideon Burnett), Luigi Pistilli (Henry Pollicut), Mario Brega (Martin), Vonetta McGee (Paulette), Jacques Dorfman (Michael), Pupita Lea Scuderoni (Michael's mother)

Music: Ennio Morricone

Plot

A fearsome gunman known as Loco leads a group of unscrupulous bounty hunters. He and his men do not hesitate to murder in cold blood those who, for whatever reason, are in search and capture. One of these fugitives is James, who in Snow Hill Village has been pushed into robbery because he cannot find work. This is because the powerful merchant and banker Pollicut, a kind of local chieftain, has sabotaged all his attempts to find honest employment. For Pollicut wants James' wife Pauline for himself.

The governor of Utah starts a crusade against the brutal and arbitrary methods of the bounty hunters. To do this, he sends to

Snow Hill Gideon Burnett, the new sheriff who will have to ensure that no abuse is committed by people like Loco. On his way to this remote village in the snowy countryside, the sheriff is ambushed by a group of outlaws. They do not intend to kill him, but simply steal his horse so they can eat. They are considered bandits, but these outcasts who live in the ever-white mountains had to leave Snow Hill after losing all their property to the usurer Pollicut. Pollicut, by the way, is the one who offers the rewards for the heads of the "bandits"; and also for James' head. Loco and others like him are always on the lookout for such rewards. In the "wanted" posters, individuals are claimed "dead or alive," and the ruthless Loco always tries to get them in the first mode - for then they no longer have a chance to defend themselves in court or try to prove their innocence.

Loco and his henchmen arrive at James' house to "stop" him. James is waiting for them with his shotgun in hand, but Loco promises that if he surrenders he will take him to the sheriff for a fair trial. James, who knows his crimes are not serious, agrees. And when he drops his gun he is shot in treason by the cruel bounty hunters, falling dead before his terrified wife Pauline. She's not willing to stand by. She has heard of a mysterious and lonely gunman who hates bounty hunters and is dedicated to eliminating them. He is nicknamed "Silence", supposedly because "wherever he goes he leaves behind only the silence of death". But there is another reason why they call him that, which Pauline does not yet know... The young widow decides to contact the enigmatic gunman, writing to an acquaintance who knows where he is.

Meanwhile, the sheriff whose horse has been stolen wanders around in the snow. When he sees a stage approaching, he signals the coachman to slow down, getting into the vehicle. Coincidentally, and fortunately for the sheriff, the stage is heading for Snow Hill. There's another passenger on board. It's Silence.

Loco is collecting the bodies of his latest victims to take them to Snow Hill and collect the rewards offered by Pollicut. He intends to take advantage of the passing of the stage to load the bodies on it. This is how he has his first encounter with Burnett, who begins to put obstacles in his way by saying that the dead should only be transported in coffins. Loco immediately realizes that the new sheriff is going to be an obstacle to his peculiar way of life. And so does the merchant Pollicut. When Pollicut sees Silence, who arrives in Snow Hill at the same time as the sheriff and Loco, he seems to recognize him. The two have already clashed in the past. The usurer orders one of his men to follow Silence and to watch his every move.

Silence heads for Pauline's house, as he has received her message and is ready to carry out the task she has given him. Pauline wants to hire him to eliminate Loco. When the widow asks him how much money he wants for the job, she is irritated at not receiving an answer. Silence then removes the kind of scarf that hides her throat, revealing a large scar on his neck: Someone slit him to remove his vocal cords and as a result he is mute. Silence writes on a piece of paper the amount he requests, 1000 dollars. Meanwhile, the gunman is welcomed as a guest in her home.

Pauline realizes that she does not have that much money, and that the only possible way to get it would be to sell her house. The only one capable of buying it would be the merchant

Pollicut - and he, as she knows, wants more from the woman than her house, something she is not willing to give him...

Commentary

It can be said that Sergio Leone is the father of the Italo-Western. Taking as a reference the stories of the West and influenced by the Japanese jidaigeki (especially Kurosawa's "Yojimbo") the Roman director developed with his Dollar Trilogy a very particular style, a style that would create a school. The solitary, hieratic and taciturn gunman became an icon of Western cinema - especially Italian-style Western cinema. The lone gunman, who used the gun as an extension of his body (just like the samurai used their swords) and who, with a very personal code of honor, wandered around the West, used to be a bounty hunter (like Clint Eastwood in the aforementioned trilogy, or Charles Bronson in "Until His Time Came"). However, as we will see, in Sergio Corbucci's film that we are dealing with today, he has a quite different perspective from the one offered in the films of his fellow countryman and namesake Leone: Leone's bounty hunter is an amoral figure, he is a mercenary beyond good and evil who only acts for money, but without showing cruelty. "The Great Silence", on the other hand, tries to "demystify" the figure of the bounty hunter; equating him to a kind of human vulture, who has made death his way of life. Leone's "bounty hunter" is amoral; but Corbucci's is a crawling villain, a despicable leech.

The setting of "The Great Silence" is the opposite of that of a regular western: no dry, dusty deserts; almost all the film takes place in the snow. Therefore, and contrary to most Italian-western films, this feature film was not shot in Almeria, but in the snowy Dolomite mountains; in the northeast of Italy.

But there is one thing that both Roman directors agree on: The protagonist is sparse with words... This characteristic had proved successful in the genre's productions. What better then, Corbucci would think, than to resort to a main character who is directly mute? And, like Harmonica in "Once upon a time in America", the protagonist has a score to settle...

Silence is not a "moral apostle" or someone who acts selflessly, for he has something personal against bounty hunters. He too, like Pauline, is motivated by revenge. These human vultures murdered his parents, using the same dirty tactic as when they killed James: telling his father to turn himself in for a fair trial, and then treacherously killing him as soon as he laid down his arms. His mother was also shot on that occasion. And in order to neutralize him, who was present as a child, the bounty hunters decided to leave him alive... but making sure, by means of a hunting knife, that he would never speak again.

The general atmosphere of the film is deeply melancholy, pessimistic and gloomy. The soundtrack by the great Ennio Morricone always enhances that feeling. But there is, of course, an alternative version with a "happy ending" that Corbucci was forced to shoot for the North African market - where the westerns were very popular but needed a less tragic conclusion.

Just as Leone took Kurosawa's Yojimbo (1961) as a reference for his "For a Fistful of Dollars" (1964), Japanese screenwriters would be inspired by "Il grande Silenzio" to create the excellent series "Oshi Samurai"/"The Mute Samurai" (1973-1974), starring Tomisaburo Wakayama.

The silent protagonist of this western is played by Frenchman Jean-Louis Trintignant. The German Klaus Kinski plays a superb role as the psychopathic Loco - a very appropriate name, although according to the version the character is also called Tigrero. African-American Vonetta McGee plays Pauline. This actress, who made her debut on camera with "Il grande Silenzio", would later appear in "Blacula" (William Crain, 1972) - "the Black Dracula", a blaxploitation of parodic terror. Luigi Pistilli (Pollicut) and Frank Wolff (the sheriff) would again be cast partners in "Milano Calibro 9" (Fernando Di Leo, 1972), the masterpiece of the polizziesco. Wolff also participated in "Once upon the time in the West" (Sergio Leone, 1968), filmed and released the same year as "Il grande Silenzio".

C'era una volta il West (a.k.a. "Once upon a time in the West")

Italy, 1968

Director: Sergio Leone

Script: Sergio Donati, Sergio Leone (based on the story of Sergio Leone, Dario Argento and Bernardo Bertolucci)

Cast: Claudia Cardinale (Jill McBain), Henry Fonda (Frank), Jason Robards (Cheyenne), Charles Bronson (Harmonica), Gabriele Ferzetti (Morton), Woody Strode (Stony)

Music: Ennio Morricone

Plot

In the far west of the USA, at the beginning of the 20th century, the first railway line is being built. Three outlaw-like individuals wait in a train station for a locomotive to arrive. Presumably they intend to rob it, but they are waiting for someone: The guy they're waiting for gets off the train, and starts playing a tune on his harmonica. He had arranged to meet a certain Frank, but this one has sent some of his men in his place. When he notices they intend to kill him, the newcomer kills them by firing his revolver.

Not far from there, Farmer Brett McBain is preparing to welcome his wife, whom he recently married. McBain has three children from his first marriage; the children's mother died six years earlier. Suddenly, the McBains' property is raided and bandits led by Frank murder the whole family: the father, the teenage son and daughter, and even the youngest son, about 7 years old.

Jill McBain arrives at the town station from New Orleans and is surprised that no one has come to pick her up. Concerned, she rides in a horse-drawn carriage to her husband's ranch. On the way, the coachman insists on stopping at a tavern. There she meets the mysterious individual with the harmonica. Soon after, the outlaw Cheyenne appears, still handcuffed, who has just escaped from the officers who were holding him. Harmonica and Cheyenne have a cross word ("Can you shoot your gun as well as play the harmonica?"), but soon the men from the second one appear and he retires with them.

Jill has witnessed the tense scene. Shortly after, she continues on to the McBain property with the horse-drawn carriage, and upon arrival discovers in horror that the entire family has been killed. Neighbors have already discovered the bodies and are keeping them on tables. The sheriff suspects the newly escaped Cheyenne and his gang of criminals of a particular piece of cloth found nearby.

Harmonica beats up a local store clerk who had been the go-between for the alleged meeting with Frank - which turned out to be a trap.

Jill decides to stay at the McBains' house instead of returning to New Orleans. The next morning she receives a visit from Cheyenne, who implies that he had nothing to do with the murders. Someone tries to frame him, having left a piece of a coat like his men wear near the scene of the crime.

Frank, meanwhile, meets with Mr. Morton, the tuberculous and invalid owner of the railroad company. It was he who had given him the task of throwing out the McBains, for the line Morton is building must pass through their property and McBain was refusing to sell it. Even so, Morton does not approve of Frank's overly violent methods, and Frank, for his part, aspires to one day get rid of Morton and control his company.

After the funeral of her husband and his children, Jill prepares to leave. But Harmonica shows up and insists that she stay. She wants to use her as bait to lure Frank out of hiding.

As McBain's widow now insists on staying there, she too becomes an obstacle. Frank sends two of his men to eliminate her. But they find that the woman is now under the protection of the enigmatic harmonica man.

Cheyenne, who has also decided to protect Jill, watches from a nearby hill as Harmonica kills Frank's henchmen. "Not only can he play the harmonica, he can also shoot," he says contentedly, referring to their first meeting at the bar.

Jill goes to the shop where Frank's mediator works, the one who arranged the false appointment for Harmonica where three of his men went instead of Frank. "Tell Frank I know everything and I'll propose him to make a deal." The employee pretends not to know Frank, but when she leaves, he goes to the train where Frank meets Morton. Harmonica was counting on it and follows him. Now he knows where her enemy is hiding. The mysterious harmonica man has a score to settle with the ruthless bandit, now in the pay of the railroad company...

Commentary

After Sergio Leone's success with his Dollar Trilogy, the Roman director planned to concentrate on his epic project about Jewish gangsters in the US (which would later crystallize into "Once Upon a Time in America", 1984), but the producers managed to convince him to shoot one more western; this time with an abundant budget and the starring participation of Henry Fonda (his favorite actor).

"Once upon a time in the West", a masterpiece of the genre, had several locations: not only the Almería desert as in the films of the Eastwood trilogy, but also Arizona, in the USA; Sonora (Mexico) and the Cinecittà studios in Rome.

Harmonica (Charles Bronson), an outsider who appears out of nowhere, joins the outlaw Cheyenne (Jason Robards) to protect the young and attractive widow Jill (Claudia Cardinale) from the fearsome and bloodthirsty Frank (Henry Fonda), who with his gang acts as a thug for the railway company run by the handicapped Morton (Gabriele Ferzetti). Jill, a former prostitute in New Orleans, had married only a month earlier the Irish rancher Brett McBain, who was planning to build a village in the desert, right where the train line was to pass. McBain and their children were fiercely murdered by Frank, as the family (who refused to leave) was a hindrance to the railway company. Cheyenne is accused of the massacre, and in order to clear his name, he sets out to find the real killers. The enigmatic Harmonica also senses that the person responsible for the atrocious crime is Frank, whom he already tries to find at all costs anyway. Frank is not content to be Morton's lackey, and waits for the right moment to eliminate him and take over his company. Morton, who is suspicious of his intentions and tired of Frank's humiliating treatment, will also try to finish him off.

The mysterious Harmonica is looking for Frank because he has an old score to settle with him. "Once upon a time in the West" is the epic story of a revenge matured over decades, which reaches its climax in the sublime scene of the duel between Harmonica and Frank (sequence masterfully accompanied by the magnificent soundtrack of Ennio Morricone and by flashback fragments that explain the motivation of Harmonica to seek revenge).

Ennio Morricone's excellent music is one of the fundamental components of the film. Several of the main characters have a characteristic musical theme, such as Cheyenne or Jill. Some years later, Morricone would take the harmonica's melody as a self-reference to include it in the thriller "Last stop on the night train" (Aldo Lado, 1975), whose soundtrack he also composed. Curiously, the plot frames of both films have to do with trains, although the respective plots as such are completely different.

Charles Bronson perfectly incarnates the classic tough guy with no name, with his paradigmatic lack of words and accurate aim, who was already brought to life by Clint Eastwood in the other westerns of Leone. Claudia Cardinale makes a great performance as Jill, a woman with a shady past whose intentions to "settle down" and embark on a placid family life are brutally cut off overnight. A great applause deserves the characterization of Henry Fonda, who gets into the boots of the cruel villain Frank.

Until the very end, Frank doesn't know who Harmonica is and what he wants from him. "Who are you?" he asks repeatedly, each time with more curiosity. Harmonica responds by giving different names each time. "But those are all dead!" "They'd be alive if they hadn't met you, Frank." Until the crucial and apotheosis duel scene, Frank doesn't know who his antagonist is, for he has so many dead people on his conscience that he doesn't know who the mysterious avenger represents...

Other memorable moments, besides the duel, are the initial scene with the bandits waiting for the train (the tension in the air is chewed), or the moments before the assault of the McBain's property (one can perceive how the sudden silence of crickets and cicadas foretells an imminent danger...)

Dario Argento, who would later become one of the greatest representatives of the giallo or Italian-style thriller, collaborated with Leone in the development of the script.

Ognuno per se, a.k.a "Every man for himself", a.k.a "Sam Cooper's gold" a.k.a "The ruthless four"

Italy, 1968

Director: Giorgio Capitano

Script: Fernando Di Leo, Augusto Caminito

Cast: Van Heflin (Sam Cooper), Gilbert Roland (Mason), Klaus Kinski (Brent the Blonde), George Hilton (Manolo Sánchez)

Music: Carlo Rustichelli

Plot

Sam Cooper and his partner Slim are digging gold out of a mine in the middle of the desert. When they've filled several sacks, greed makes Slim a traitor. He tries to kill Sam, but he's quicker and gets his opponent killed. Leaving the body there, Sam sets out to return to the village from which he left. But he can't take all the gold by himself. And there's still a whole left in the mine. Sam buries some sacks of gold nearby, and crosses the desert to the village.

Once there he meets up again with his friend Ann, to whom he explains that he has found the mine; but he needs a partner to help him with the excavations and the transport of the precious metal. The problem is that finding someone you can trust is almost impossible. All the partners who have accompanied him on his expeditions so far have ended up turning against him, blinded by greed. Sam realizes that the only person he can trust is young Manolo, who is a kind of son to him - because Sam lived with his mother in the past. The veteran miner sends Manolo a telegram to come there immediately. The boy has always been very honest and unambitious, characteristics that make him an ideal partner.

Soon Manolo arrives from Denver. As they have not seen each other for years, Sam is a little ambiguous at first; without suddenly revealing his discovery. But little by little, he begins to show that he has found a gold mine and that he needs an assistant. He is willing to share half of the profits with him. Once the alcohol has flowed copiously, Sam even explains to him the area of the desert where the treasure is located.

In the village, there are some disturbing figures. Among them are the Brady brothers, who are hired killers. Then there's Mason, Sam's contemporary and a former army buddy. Years ago, they were both involved in a robbery, and only Mason was arrested. Since then, Mason has held a certain grudge against Sam, suspecting he was betrayed. On a stormy night, a dark blond rider with an icy look arrives in town and keeps an eye on young Manolo. He seems to have followed him there. Manolo shudders at the sight of him in the saloon, but in Sam's face he pretends not to recognize him. Ann notices something strange and tells Sam that she suspects Manolo. Maybe it wasn't such a good idea to think of him as a partner...

One night, Sam wakes up and notices that Manolo's bed is empty. He hears voices in the hallway and sees the young man talking to the strange blond man. Manolo tells Sam that he will accompany them. When the miner is angry, he explains that this individual, who wears the habits of a priest and is called "the

Reverend", has been his "protector" for the last few years (since Sam left his mother); and that for this he is indebted to him. Manolo assures Sam that he will not have losses, since the Reverend will be paid 50% of his share.

Very disappointed by Manolo's attitude, Sam decides he needs someone to watch his back. And he thinks of Mason for that. He hopes to make peace with him by promising him 10% of the loot they get from the mine. But Mason claims half his share.

So, after buying supplies, sleeping bags and digging equipment, the four of them set off for the mine. But everyone is suspicious of each other, no one trusts the other three, they are always on guard, fearing some dirty trick by one of the "partners"...

At first they are held together because of an ambush they suffer (one of the assailants turns out to be the shop assistant where they bought the equipment), but from the moment they arrive at the mine and start digging, the conspiratorial atmosphere and mutual distrust prevail. Moreover, a sheriff is on the prowl: He is looking for a thief and murderer who, as a fugitive from justice, flees disguised as a reverend...

Commentary

This is a very well-constructed western, where the development of the characters, as well as the suspense and tension, increase the spectator's interest as the minutes go by. The plot is solid, the violence forceful, and instead of revealing explicitly several details only alludes (as the past of the Reverend and his relationship with Manolo, who seems to depend on him, feeling somehow under coercion) which gives the movie an aura of mystery that makes it superior to the stereotypical western.

The high quality of the story is most probably due to the fact that it was co-written by the great Fernando Di Leo - one of the scriptwriters who collaborated with Sergio Leone in the "Dollar Trilogy", who would later direct his own films, specializing in the polizziesco sub-genre and making titles such as "Milano Calibro 9" (1972) or "Il Boss" (1973).

The plot is reminiscent of the classic western "The treasure of the Sierra Madre" (John Huston, 1948).

"Ognuno per se" is an Italian-German co-production (that's why the credits are in German), and like countless other westerns it was shot in Almería (Spain).

Sam Cooper is played by the US-American Van Heflin, who had already participated in several American westerns. This is also the case with Gilbert Roland, who brings Mason to life. Roland was of Mexican origin and his real name was Luis Antonio Dámaso de Alonso. The charismatic Klaus Kinski plays the sinister "Reverend". Kinski already shone in similar psychopathic roles in spaghetti-western gems like "Il grande Silenzio" (Sergio Corbucci, 1968), shot by the way that same year. Uruguayan George Hilton (pseudonym of Jorge Hill Acosta) plays Manolo. This actor participated with Franco Nero in "Massacre time", a memorable contribution to the genre by the master Lucio Fulci (and also scripted by Fernando Di Leo).

The soundtrack was composed by Carlo Rustichelli and directed by Bruno Nicolai, who by the way collaborated with Ennio Morricone.

Due volte Giuda, a.k.a. "They were called Graveyard"

Italy, 1969

Director: Nando Cicero

Script: Jaime Jesús Balcázar

Cast: Klaus Kinski (Dingus), Antonio Sabato (Luke Barrett)

Music: Carlos Pes

Plot

In the arid desert, a man who begins to be pecked by vultures awakens from his unconsciousness. Next to him lies a corpse. Once he has regained his senses, he shoots the birds of prey to drive them away. An old man crossing the burning sands towards the nearest town watches the funny scene.

The young man who has woken up asks him what has happened, for he does not remember anything. He does not know who he is or how he got there. He doesn't know who the dead man is, now eaten by the vultures; probably his companion in misfortune. Everything indicates that they were both attacked. He managed to survive, but suffers from an amnesia that prevents him from remembering his identity and what he was doing before he was knocked out.

The amnesiac arrives at the village hall, where he is recognized by an individual who was waiting for him. "You're late, Luke," he says. He also asks for the whereabouts of one Donovan (Luke imagines that it is his dead companion in the desert). The character in the saloon had summoned them for a job: A certain Victor Barrett is to be killed.

This Victor Barrett is an influential inhabitant of the town, a benefactor of many Mexicans who cross the border into the United States. Barrett is trying to prevent local residents from selling their land and property to the bank. For that reason, he has a confrontation with Murphy, the local banker.

He is determined to acquire the land at a low price and to drive the owners out of the area.
As planned, Luke sets out to kill Barrett. The man who hired him has his back from a nearby hill. Luke is recognised by Barrett and those with him. Everyone thought he died during the recent Civil War. Instead of fulfilling his assignment, Luke decides at the last minute to save Barrett's life, pushing him to the ground and dodging the shots of the individual shooting from the top of the hill. After an exchange of bullets, he is killed by Luke. The amnesiac, who still remembers nothing, is taken to the sheriff's office cell, but is soon released through the intercession of Victor Barrett. This happens to be Luke's older brother.

Victor continues his lawsuit with banker Murphy, who tries to scare off the locals and buy their property. Barrett insists that no one sell their homes or land to the bank.

Luke learns from his sick mother that he was married and his wife was about to give birth to a son, but that she died shortly before. His brother Victor, whom he asks about the event, tells him that his wife was killed by Yankee soldiers during the war; but investigating on his own, Luke discovers that a certain Dingus is responsible for the tragedy...

Commentary

As interesting as the story is about an amnesiac gunman in the West who tries to remember his past and discovers a crime he decides to take revenge on, the good idea of the plot is neither well used nor well implemented, making the plot confusing and tiring.

Nor does the presence of two greats like Klaus Kinski (in the role of Victor Barrett) and Narciso Ibáñez Menta (as Murphy) manage to save the film. This Nando Cicero's italo-western written by the Balcázar brothers is really a disappointment.

The plot itself is promising, and has vast potential to generate intrigue and suspense; in fact it would have been possible to include elements of giallo in this western. But the narrative pace unfortunately leaves something to be desired, making the film a tedious and mediocre display of the sub-genre.

However, "Due volte Giuda" is not completely to be dismissed. There is some tension in the atmosphere: The viewer senses that Victor Barret (Kinski) has a lot to hide, and that he is not really the selfless, altruistic benefactor he might at first seem to be. His amnesiac brother Luke also suspects that Victor has not told him the whole truth, and even that he has something to do with this Dingus...

Night of the Serpent

Italy, 1969

Director: Giulio Petroni

Script: Giulio Petronio, Fulvio Gicca Palli, Lorenzo Gicca Palli

Cast: Luke Askew (Luke), Luigi Pistilli (Lieutenant Hernández), Magda Konopka (María), Chelo Alonso (Dolores), Benito Stefanelli (Pancho)

Music: Riz Ortolani

Plot

One stormy night, in a small Mexican town, telegraphist Martín dies after being beaten by Mayor Venustiano and innkeeper Ignacio. Both leave the body at the side of a road to make it look like an accident and take the message that Martín was about to telegraph. Lieutenant Hernández senses that the death is not a mere misfortune due to the storm. He immediately suspects Venustiano and Ignacio. Furthermore, he finds a copy of the telegram; it incriminates both of them as well as the prostitute Dolores and the sacristan Jesús María. The four are relatives of each other, and were conspiring to get the money of the disappeared bandit León Carrizo. Lieutenant Hernández blackmails them, saying he knows everything. In exchange for not sending them to the gallows he presses them to join them

and become part of the plot. The group's goal is to eliminate
León Carrizo's son, who could claim the dollars they plan to
take over.

Hernández goes to the hideout of Pancaldo, leader of a gang of
revolutionaries and criminals. He asks him to hand over one of
his henchmen, one who is useful but not worth much, since after
fulfilling his mission he will be immediately captured and
executed to settle the matter. Pancaldo offers him Luke, an
alcoholic gringo he picked up months earlier in the desert.

Luke is a finished man. In the past he had been an expert
gunman, but because of his drinking addiction and a trauma he
suffered he is no longer even a shadow of what he was. His
hands are shaking. Pancaldo considers him "a dead man who
walks", he is cannon fodder, willing to do anything for a shot of
tequila.

When Luke arrives at the village, he goes to Ignacio's inn and is
immediately arrested as he is considered a vagabond. Hernández
releases him, realizing that he is the man sent by Pancaldo. Luke
stays around the tavern waiting for instructions. He becomes
friends with the boy Manuel, Ignacio's assistant. Seeing that
Luke has nowhere to sleep, the young man invites him to his
house, where he lives with the healer María, his adoptive
mother.

Thanks to her, and to his own willpower, Luke begins to
overcome his alcoholism. He soon realizes that the person he
must kill, Carrizo's son, is none other than little Manuel. Luke
refuses, and in a disciplined way he exercises his aim to defend
himself from Pancaldo's bandits, and from the town's

conspirators (the mayor, the prostitute, the innkeeper and the sacristan), who in addition to being cousins to each other are related to Manuel and are now led by the evil Lieutenant Hernández.

Commentary

A good western whose plot bases are, on the one hand, a conspiracy and, on the other, the striving to improve of the protagonist; a gunman who, at first, is unable to hit a single shot but later recovers the skill he had before falling into the vice of drinking. In this sense, it is very interesting to mention the deep symbolic charge of the scene where Luke changes hats: First he wears a shattered straw hat, full of holes, which effectively makes him look like a beggar; then he wears an elegant cowboy hat. Then he shoots a bottle of tequila, getting it the first try. The bottle is no longer a temptation for him, but an object that helps him to regain his skill with the gun.

The film was directed by Giulio Petroni, director of the western "Death rides a horse" (1967). That film too begins, curiously, with a stormy night. Lieutenant Hernández is played by Luigi Pistilli, who we saw in "The big Silence" (Sergio Corbucci, 1968), in "The killers are our guests" (Vincenzo Rigo, 1974) or in minor roles in "For a few dollars more" (1965) or "The good, the bad and the ugly" (1966), both by Sergio Leone. Dolores is embodied by the Cuban Chelo Alonso, who during the 1950s and early 1960s had been "the queen of the peplum" in productions such as "Goliath and the Barbarians" (1959) or "Atlas in the land of the Cyclops" (1961). This "Night of the Serpent" was her last participation in the world of cinema.

The soundtrack was composed by Riz Ortolani, and some of its chords are reminiscent of the music that the same author would later create for the giallo "Don´t torture a duckling" (Lucio Fulci, 1972).

Django the Bastard

Italy, 1969

Filmaker: Sergio Garrone

Script: Sergio Garrone, Anthony Steffen

Cast: Anthony Steffen (Django), Paolo Gozlino (Mayor Rod Murdock), Jean Louis (Ross), Rada Rassimov (Alethea / Alida)
Music: Vasily Kokhucharov, Elsio Mancuso

Plot

A lonely stranger dressed in black arrives in an arid village, armed with his revolver and a wooden cross on which is written a name (that of a Hawkins) and a date (that day). Rough gunmen see him arrive from the saloon. They are Hawkins' cronies. Hawkins, alerted by his own people, goes out to meet the stranger, who threateningly shows him the cross that bears his name. Before the stunned Hawkins can react, the stranger pulls out his revolver and riddles him with bullets, leaving the wooden cross nailed to his body.

Hawkins will not be the only one to be killed by the shots of the enigmatic gunman in black. A new wooden cross, this time with the name "Ross" and the date of the next day, is entrusted to an undertaker by the mysterious character, called Django. One by one, his enemies fall, those with whom Django intends to settle accounts, to settle murky affairs of the past.

The local rancher and chieftain, Rod Murdock, fears more than anyone else the revenge of the mysterious and lethal stranger. So he gathers a group of henchmen to hunt him down. Meanwhile, Django continues to execute his revenge. Murdock's henchmen seem unable to stop him...

Commentary

Routine western where a lone gunman, with sinister airs and a supernatural aura, seeks revenge on his enemies - who believe him dead. The protagonist has "returned from hell" to exact his revenge. The background and the concrete reasons for such revenge, related to the American civil war in which Django was a soldier, will be revealed towards the end, with the usual use of flashbacks: During the fight, his superior Murdock left his men in the lurch, betraying his loyal soldiers... One of them was Django, who promised himself not to rest until he found Murdock and his henchmen, executing them one by one.

On the whole, the proposal brings nothing new to the genre. Both the plot and the style are analogous to most of the Italo-Western products of those years. The title and the name of the main character seek to exploit the commercial success of Corbucci's "Django" played by Franco Nero, without the film being a sequel.

If the original Django is characterized by dragging a coffin, the one in the film is dedicated to carrying crosses on which are written the names of his enemies and the expected date of their respective deaths (crosses that he nails to the ground next to the bodies once his revenge has been consummated).

This Django is embodied by Anthony Steffen, who we saw in the disappointing giallo "The Night Evelyn Came Out of the Grave" (Emilio Miraglia, 1971) and in the lesser-known thriller "Tropic of Cancer" (Edoardo Mulargia, 1972). Steffen collaborated with director Sergio Garrone in the development of the script.

The soundtrack, quite average and not very memorable, was composed by the Bulgarian Vasili Kojucharov; who, on the other hand, was the author of the music of the much more interesting but underrated "Byleth: The Demon of Incest" (Leopoldo Savona, 1972).

My name is Shanghai Joe

Italy, 1973

Director: Mario Caiano

Script: Mario Caiano, Carlo Alberto Alfieri

Cast: Chen Lee (Shanghai Joe), Klaus Kinski (Scalper Jack),
Gordon Mitchell (Burying Sam), Carla Romanelli (Cristina)

Music: Bruno Nicolai

Plot

Around 1870, numerous Chinese immigrants arrived in San
Francisco. One of them is known as "Shanghai Joe", who soon
suffers from the racism of the "WASP". The Chinese Joe, a
young man dressed in the style of his country, including a
ponytail, travels to Texas, where he unsuccessfully seeks work
as a cowboy.

He tries to get a job on a ranch, but the cowboys in charge make
fun of him, taunt him and think they can ridicule him by
subjecting him to certain tests. Joe is victorious, showing off his
acrobatic skills and driving a nail into a wood without a
hammer, and then he claims his reward: a horse. But the
cowboys are not willing to give him what he has earned, and try
to humiliate him with a whip.

The Chinese, however, are experts in kung fu, and easily
manage to reduce their opponents to escape on the back of the

promised horse. He later stays at a boarding house, where a family of thugs (consisting of the elderly father and his four rude offspring) also stay there and challenge him to a poker game.

The Chinese man is an absolute winner, and takes the money that the others had bet. His opponents try to recover what they lost during the night, preparing to attack Joe while he sleeps. But he wakes up in time and thanks to his martial arts mastery he beats them all to a pulp.

After that, he continues his search for a job in the Wild West, and is approached not much later by some enigmatic horsemen who promise him a good job. They have heard of his combat skills and are interested in hiring him to "look after cattle". Soon after, Joe realizes that the "cattle" these individuals were referring to is a group of Mexican prisoners, sold by an equally Mexican outlaw for use as slaves. Joe remains astonished, for he believed that slavery had already been abolished in the United States.

When the authorities then come to carry out some kind of raid, the bandits "free" the Mexicans (so that they cannot be accused of slave trade), only to shoot them while they try to hide ("so that there is no evidence left"). In the face of this cowardly and crawling procedure, Joe reacts with indignation and tries to neutralize the criminals who had hired him through kung fu. This is how some of the prisoners manage to save themselves. One of them is an old man, who is later taken care of by Joe, after which he can return home.

The slave traders, however, manage to capture Joe and take him to their boss, a cruel and ruthless rancher with whom the sheriff of the area is in league. There, they throw the Chinese man into a bullring, and release a wild boar, who tries to ram him several times. But Joe always dodges it, to the amazement of his enemies, and even manages to kick it off after performing an acrobatic pirouette. Then, leaving his opponents speechless, he sits down in the saddle of a horse and takes the chief of the bandits, the evil rancher, hostage.

Once away from his domain, the cowardly rancher begs for his life, pleading for mercy. Joe spares his life after hitting him a couple of times and leaves. Not killing that enemy when he could have done so will bring him new problems, for the rancher, instead of forgetting his differences with the Chinese man, will put a price on his head.

Joe denounces the chief slave trader to the sheriff of the county, but this is a corrupt man who is in the service of the influential landowner. The sheriff, instead of arresting the criminal, tries to imprison the Chinese man for "defamation" and "horse stealing," but the speedy Joe manages to escape in time, and, disappointed, continues on his way.

He arrives at a new boarding house, after meeting an attractive young Mexican woman named Cristina along the way, who turns out to be the daughter of the old man Joe helped from the slavers. The Chinese man and the girl become friends, and from now on he will become her protector.

The girl is kidnapped the next morning (while Joe was still sleeping in the stable, because there wasn't enough room in the inn), and the Oriental wannabe cowboy will go to great lengths to rescue her. The abductor is a disturbing character who has set a trap with sharp stakes. Thanks to his prodigious reflexes, Joe manages to save himself from a horrific death, and after a hand-to-hand struggle where the Asian has a clear advantage, the evil opponent ends up being the victim of his own trap. Joe releases Cristina, after a new confrontation with a quirky cannibal and his alcoholic comrade.

But the girl is ill, affected by high fevers, and the brave Chinese must find a doctor. The dangers continue, the enemies lie in wait, and there are many who are willing to capture Shanghai Joe to collect the reward offered by the evil rancher...

Commentary

A curious Italo-Western with an oriental (or Italo-Eastern?) flavour, whose protagonist is a Chinese man who has recently arrived in the arid Texan countryside in search of a job as a cowboy. But he's not just any Chinese guy, he's a kung-fu expert, who doesn't let himself be intimidated by the rough cowboys and with his acrobatic kicks is almost as fast as the bullets the gunmen fire from their revolvers.

The actor who plays Chinese Joe is Chen Lee, a martial artist who also appeared in other action films. The film features the participation of the illustrious Klaus Kinski, and a very good soundtrack by Bruno Nicolai (who composed the music for Jesús Franco's adaptation of the Marquis de Sade's "Justine" or Tinto Brass' "Caligula").

"Shanghai Joe" seeks to highlight the racism and discrimination traditionally practiced by the Anglo-Saxons (perhaps exaggerating it a bit); it also features moments of black humor (characteristic of Italian western films) and a good dose of violence (for example, when Chinese Joe rips out one of his opponents' eyes during a fight in the saloon).

It's an interesting film for lovers of the genre, but it's obviously not up to the masterpieces of Leone or Corbucci. Being an atypical Italo-Western it reminds of films like Ferdinando Baldi's "Blindman" (1971) (about a blind gunman, which in turn is reminiscent of the blind Japanese swordsman Zatoichi). Director Mario Caiano made, among other films, the polizziesco "Napoli spara!" (1976) with Henry Silva.

An army of five men (O. V. Un esercito di 5 uomini)

Italy, 1969

Director: Don Taylor, Italo Zingarelli

Script: Marc Richards, Dario Argento

Cast: Peter Graves (Dutch), James Daly (Augustus), Bud Spencer (Mesito), Nino Castelnuovo (Luis Domínguez), Tetsuro Tanba (Samurai), Marno Masé (Railway Man), Daniela Giordano (Maria), Pietro Torrisi (Mexican Officer)

Music: Ennio Morricone

Plot

Luis, a Mexican bandit, begins to recruit several individuals to make a coup: First the big Mesito, who has retired from the

119

world of crime and works on a farm. Then Augustus, a veteran explosives expert turned professional card sharpener. And finally a Japanese man known as "the Samurai," who puts on knife-throwing shows for a traveling theater company. Luis takes them to "the Dutchman", who has hatched a plan to get his hands on a large amount of gold.

The five cross the border into Mexico and head for a town whose inhabitants are being suppressed by General Huerta's army. The group led by the Dutchman intervenes before the soldiers begin to shoot the insurgents, saving the leader of the rebels: the peasant Manuel Esteban. He knows that Huerta will soon receive a shipment of gold from his European allies. The revolutionary intends to get hold of the precious metal with the help of the five bandits. The Dutchman has forged an alliance with the rebels and to strike, he needs the collaboration of Luis, Augustus, Mesito and the Samurai. This "army of five men" will have to face the Mexican military who, heavily armed, guard the train on which the gold is transported.

The Dutchman has planned the assault on the train down to the last detail, and is instructing his men to execute the ambitious project. Augustus believes that this is a suicide mission, that they have no chance of surviving. But since he has nothing left to lose anyway, he agrees to collaborate.

As they prepare to act, they are arrested by Captain Gutiérrez's men, for having saved the revolutionary Esteban from being shot. They are locked in a cell, but manage to escape thanks to the help of a young Mexican woman (who passed a knife to the Samurai). Once again, they are free and they go over the last details of the coup. They are dressed in Mexican soldiers' uniforms so that they can infiltrate the military that is guarding the shipment, and everything is ready for action...

Commentary

Like many other Italian westerns, this production is set in the context of Mexican revolutionary upheavals. As the central theme is the assault on a train, the footage is full of shoot-outs, explosions and fights, which gives the film a rather fast pace, thus combining the most conventional western cinema with the adventure genre. The plot is slightly inspired by the warlike "The dirty dozen" (Robert Aldrich, 1967) and the American western "The Magnificent Seven" (John Sturges, 1960).

Dario Argento, who would later achieve worldwide fame with his bloody and stylized thrillers, co-wrote this entertaining western. A certain enigma surrounds the authorship of the direction: American Don Taylor is listed as the director in the English version of the film, but according to other versions the film would have been directed by producer Italo Zingarelli. It seems that the shooting was started by one of them and finished by the other. Some even claim that Dario Argento himself was involved as a co-director.

As for the cast, the famous Bud Spencer stands out, playing Mesito. As "Samurai" we have one of the most emblematic actors of the chambara/jidaigeki (a genre quite similar to the western): Tetsuro Tanba, who we saw in "Seppuku" (Masaki Kobayashi, 1962) and in "Bohachi Bushido" (Teruo Ishii, 1973). In the role of Luis is Nino Castelnuovo, who would participate in the interesting giallo "Strip nude for your killer" (Andrea Bianchi, 1975). In a minor role appears Miss Italy 1966 Daniela

Giordano (as the Mexican who helps outlaws to escape), who we know from an horror film set in Egypt, "Shadow of Illusion" (Mario Caiano, 1970). There are also short appearances of Marino Masé (the Pignataro from "Il Boss" by Fernando Di Leo, 1973) and Pietro Torrisi (future protagonist of Italian-style barbarian films such as "Gunan" by Franco Prosperi, 1982).

The very remarkable soundtrack was composed by the master Ennio Morricone.

Mátalo! (Kill him!)

Italy, 1970

Director: Cesare Canevari

Script: Mino Roli, Nico Ducci, Eduardo Manzanos

Cast: Lou Castel (Ray), Corrado Pani (Burt), Claudia Gravy (Mary)

Music: Mario Migliardi

Plot

Bart, a dangerous criminal, is about to be executed. On the scaffold, and with the rope already tightening on his throat, he still maintains his insolent and defiant attitude, mocking the situation. Suddenly, several men start shooting from the rooftops. They are Mexican bandits who intervene to free the prisoner. The prisoner takes possession of a sack full of gold, but a mysterious woman dressed in black cannot stop him. Bart escapes on horseback with the Mexicans. The bandits prepare to separate at the border from the condemned man they have saved from death, and Bart gives them the gold as payment. But moments later, he treacherously shoots them in the back and takes the precious metal again. It's his curious way of showing his "appreciation".

Soon after, Bart is reunited with two of his buddies, Ray and Ted. The three of them head to Colorado, passing by a cemetery where the graves of people named "Benson" abound. The outlaws arrive in a ghost town and settle in the abandoned local boarding house. Mary, one of the outlaws' girlfriends and a frequent accomplice in the outlaw trio's troubled lives, soon joins them.

The next day the four of them assault a stagecoach, mercilessly murdering its occupants. Only one child is left alive, and he is allowed to escape on horseback. During the shooting Bart is hit by some shots and his companions leave him for dead. Thus the loot to be distributed is greater for each of the three remaining.

Ray, Ted and Mary, with the stolen gold, set out to rest in the ghost town before they make their next coup. But after a strange fire, an old woman appears there, claiming to be the owner of the house and the only survivor of the Benson family. Soon a young blonde and an exhausted, thirsty man arrive separately in the desolate, barren landscape. The outlaws brutally interrogate the unknown couple, for they do not believe that their appearance is fortuitous. Meanwhile, someone else lurks in the abandoned village's bell tower, armed with a shotgun...

Commentary

Interesting and unknown sample of the most violent and visceral Italo-Western. It highlights a style sometimes typical of a horror film accompanied by a highly memorable soundtrack (composed by Mario Migliardi). This soundtrack ranges from experimental music based on synthesizers to progressive rock and sound effects which could be classified as "dark-ambient" - which contributes to give the product its oppressive and disturbing atmosphere.

The psychopathic and sardonic Bart, an unscrupulous individual who, after murdering the Mexicans who saved him from death by hanging, presents himself through the use of voiceover, is very reminiscent of the type of characters that Klaus Kinski used to play in the films of this sub-genre. It also reminds us of Tomas Milian in his most sadistic and ruthless way - as in Fulci´s "The Four of the Apocalypse", which would not see the light of day until five years later. Bart is incarnated by a superb Corrado Pani, who from the first moment we see him with the rope around his neck, cynical and indifferent to death, manages to radiate a magnetic charisma. The femme fatale Mary is played by Claudia Gravy, whom we saw in the underrated "Byleth: the Demon of incest" (Leopoldo Savona, 1972). This Belgian actress was born in the Congo when it was still a colony and has lived in Spain since the 1960s. She had a minor role in the adaptation to the big screen of "Justine" by the Marquis de Sade, carried out by Jesús Franco in 1969.

This film is not the only one that successfully combines Western cinema with elements of the horror genre, and the resources employed in terms of camera handling and photography remain in the canons of the more classic Italian-Western: Zooms abound, close-ups to the eyes, it focuses on several occasions directly on the sun to highlight the torridity of the desert and the ghost town - which at night, by the way, acquires a sinister and disturbing aura.

There are few short dialogues, as is usually the case in "spaghetti-western", and as an innovation we have the use of the boomerang as a weapon - and not just the usual revolvers. "Mátalo!" was filmed in Almería and presented at the San Sebastian film festival.

Director Cesare Canevari, with nine films to his credit, began his career in westerns but ended up opting for exploitation and softcore.

The four of the Apocalypse (VO: I quattro dell'Apocalisse)

Italy, 1975

Filmaker: Lucio Fulci

Script: Ennio De Concini, Lucio Fulci (based on stories by Bret Harte)

Performers: Fabio Testi (Stubby), Lynne Frederick (Bunny), Michael J. Pollard (Clem), Harry Baird (Bud), Tomas Milian (Chaco)

Music: Franco Bixio, Fabio Frizzi, Vince Tempera

Plot

Utah, 1873. The professional gambler Stubby Preston arrives in the town of Salt Flats with the intention of working in the saloon-casino. However, he is immediately arrested by the sheriff, who throws his deck of cards on the fire and throws him in the dungeon. There, Stubby meets three other inmates: the young prostitute Bunny (who is pregnant), a slightly deranged black man named Bud, and the hardcore alcoholic Clem.

That same night, a violent assault on the saloon takes place. Masked men shoot at everyone there, at the passivity of the sheriff - who was undoubtedly in league with the perpetrators of the massacre. Thus Stubby was lucky to find himself locked in a cell, and it can be said that by locking him up the sheriff saved his life.

The next day the player and his three captive companions are released. Crossing the desert in a horse-drawn carriage they head for the next town. On the way they meet a caravan of settlers from Switzerland who belong to a Protestant sect similar to the Mormons or the Amish. The contrast between the members of the congregation, so devout and strictly religious, and the "four of the apocalypse" (one who earns his living thanks to gambling, one who rents her body, a drunkard who does not hesitate to drink cologne and a madman) is striking. Obviously Stubby doesn't reveal to the Swiss what they really do, and he and Bunny pretend to be husband and wife. Stubby notes that the evangelists are unarmed, and therefore unprotected; but the leader of the group claims that they have "God's weapons".

The time comes to separate from the settlers and the four continue their journey. They notice the arrival of a group of bandits but have time to hide. They realize that this is a dangerous area, full of outlaws and Indians. It's not just the Amish who are in danger: they are, too.

During Bunny's birthday celebration a bullet hits the canteen Stubby was drinking from. The gunman approaches the group: Chaco, a Mexican gunman. The disturbing individual offers to protect them ("I am a good hunter"), in exchange for traveling with them in his horse-drawn carriage. Stubby decides to accept. For some time everything works out well. Chaco has great skill with firearms and thanks to his marksmanship they never lack food. The Mexican also repels some riders who ride threateningly towards them. He kills three of them and wounds a fourth, who happens to be a sheriff. Chaco tortures him sadistically, in front of his perplexed fellow travelers. Stubby considers this to be unnecessary cruelty.

At night, Chaco offers peyote to Stubby, Bunny and Bud. To Clem he promises alcohol instead. They don't suspect the real intentions of the Mexican: Obnubate them by means of the hallucinogenic cactus to leave them out of combat and steal their scarce belongings and the horse-drawn carriage, abandoning them in the desert. Chaco uses Clem to tie up his friends in exchange for the promised alcohol. Anxious to soak his throat, the drunkard obeys without complaint. But Stubby is not completely drugged and sees Chaco take advantage of this to abuse the unconscious Bunny. That ignites his anger. When Clem understands what has happened, realizing how he has been used by Chaco, he tries to hit him with a stone but the bandit shoots him in the leg; and he leaves, abandoning the four of them in the torrid sands without water or provisions.

Stubby manages to free himself from his bonds, and with the other three he continues his march. Clem is badly wounded, and Bunny's condition is becoming more and more delicate with her pregnancy.

Stubby's main objective now is not to reach the next village, but to find Chaco to settle the score. After a few more days on the road, the four of them are moved by a shocking discovery: the bodies of the members of the evangelist community next to those who traveled some time ago; dozens of human bodies grazed by vultures. A horrendous carnage; innocent men, women and children bloodily slaughtered.

Stubby is convinced that after such a massacre there can only be one responsible: Chaco. And he swears vengeance to make him pay for his crimes...

Commentary

This late Fulcian western has a reputation as one of the most violent films of the subgenre. The story is not an original idea of Fulci or of the scriptwriter Ennio De Concini (author of the brilliant plot of the first seasons of "La Piovra"), but it is based on two stories of US-American author Bret Harte, specialized in adventures with a western theme.

Lucio Fulci, who in the following years would dedicate himself almost exclusively to horror and dark, lurid and macabre themes, had previously directed another memorable western: "Massacre Time" (1966), starring Franco Nero and superior in my opinion to this "The Four of the Apocalypse".

Explicit violence is a constant, especially since the appearance of the sadistic Chaco (who, among other atrocities, slowly skinned a sheriff with the metallic tip of his star-plate). Tomas Milian, the actor in charge of playing the brutal bandit, declared that he was inspired by Charles Manson to play this character. And it's true that in his appearance, gestures and body language, Chaco is quite reminiscent of the instigator of the insane murder of Sharon Tate. The use of peyote, as an analogue to the LSD so in vogue in the hippy-satanic scene of the last 60's, could be another parallelism between the film's villain and Manson.

The surreal and hypnotic atmosphere of the ghost town and the cemetery is very well achieved. It is a small foretaste of what

Fulci would bring us a few years later with gems of dreamlike and Lovecraftian horror such as "The Beyond" (1981) and "City of the Livind Dead" (1980).

Stabby is embodied by Fabio Testi, whom we saw in excellent polizzieschi thrillers like "Revolver" (Sergio Sollima, 1973) or "The big racket" (Enzo G. Castellari, 1976). Bunny is played by British actress Lynne Frederick, who would die tragically at the age of 39 as a result of alcohol and drug abuse.

The soundtrack is composed by Fabio Frizzi, author of the masterful music of the aforementioned "The Beyond" and "City of the livind dead". And also by Vince Tempera, who also collaborated with Fulci in "The house of clocks" (1989). Considering the very high level of these composers (especially Frizzi) the work they did on "The Four of the Apocalypse" is somewhat disappointing.

Keoma

Italy, 1976

Director: Enzo G. Castellari

Script: Enzo G. Castellari, George Eastman, Mino Roli, Nico Ducci, Joshua Sinclair

Cast: Franco Nero (Keoma Shannon), William Berger (William Shannon), Olga Karlatos (Liza Farrow), Orso Maria Guerrini (Butch Shannon), Donald O'Brien (Caldwell)

Music: Guido De Angelis, Maurizio De Angelis

Plot

Keoma, a long-haired and long-bearded gunman, returns after many years to his hometown. There he finds that a ruthless gang of thugs, led by Caldwell, now controls the population. These are the years following the American civil war, and in some areas of the country there are still power gaps, which are exploited by unscrupulous people.

On the outskirts of the village, Keoma sees a caravan full of detainees crossing the meadows. Caldwell's men have captured several people suffering from a kind of plague, to confine them somewhere remote. The disease would be easily cured with medicine, but Caldwell, who is trying to squeeze every last penny out of the locals, wants to charge exorbitant prices for introducing the drugs. Thanks to the plague, which has spread after drinking bad water, Caldwell can subject the villagers to his will. His gunmen make sure that no one crosses the town line without his permission.

Several of the sick people in the caravan try to escape, but are shot by Caldwell's henchmen. Among the victims is the husband of Liza, a pregnant woman who witnessed the massacre. Also Keoma, from a nearby mound, witnesses everything. And he intervenes to rescue Liza, easily killing several of Caldwell's men.

With Liza, Keoma arrives at the village hall; where he asks for accommodation for the woman. Several of the people present recognize her as one of the sick, and Keoma must once again use his gun to prevent them from being thrown out. After many years, Keoma sees old George again, a former slave whom he had known since his childhood and for whom he had great admiration. Now, despite being a free man, George has fallen into depression and alcoholism.

Keoma heads to the ranch where he grew up. There he meets up again with his father, William Shannon. Keoma is his illegitimate son, the result of his relationship with an Indian woman. Shannon has three other children from his marriage: Butch, Sam and Lenny. They always hated Keoma for being a "half-breed bastard". Now they're part of the gang of the "strongest guy in the place": Caldwell.

At first alone, but later also with the help of his father and George, Keoma will try to protect Liza, get the medicines to the sick and free the people from the "warlord" Caldwell and his henchmen - including his own brothers...

Commentary

Just when spaghetti-western seemed to have given its last gasp, this "Keoma" was released with great success; resurrecting the sub-genre and giving rise to a new wave of twilight films from the Italian production west - among them also the memorable "Mannaja" (1977) by Sergio Martino. Ten years after characterizing "Django", Franco Nero would once again step into the shoes of a wandering gunman; who besides handling colt divinely demonstrates great skill in throwing knives.

This time it is the mestizo Keoma, who returning from fighting in the American civil war must now face another fratricidal conflict - in the literal sense. His three brothers, who despise him for being illegitimate and for being half Indian (although one of them seems more "Indian" than he is, by the way) are in the opposite trench; for they support the cruel chieftain Caldwell (but we will see that the Shannon's loyalty to their chief is not unbreakable, and that they actually plan to supplant him).

Keoma is first and foremost a lover of freedom (this will be demonstrated especially in the end: "He cannot die because he is a free man, and free men are immortal").) He soon realizes that the villagers, including George and the doctor, are too pusillanimous to face Caldwell and his gang on their own, and are initially unwilling to take any chances to win their freedom, but he manages to inspire them to break through the siege imposed on them.

"Keoma" has great parallels with "Django". We also have the female figure that the protagonist takes under his wing. In this case it is Liza, played by Olga Karlatos - who a few years later would become famous thanks to the splinter in the eye scene in "Zombi 2" (Lucio Fulci, 1979). The moment when Keoma and Liza arrive at the saloon, when the manager tells them that there are no rooms available and Keoma forces one of the prostitutes present to give him her key is reminiscent of an identical situation in "Django". Both films were produced by Manolo Bolognini.

Several scenes are worth noting, including Keoma's "flashbacks" when he arrives at his father's ranch and sees himself being beaten up by his three brothers as a child. Also the protagonist's confrontation with four of Caldwell's gunmen: When they tell him that he must pay a tribute for the medicines that enter the village, Keoma responds that he will pay four cents - the price of four bullets (one for each of them...)

In "Keoma" symbolism abounds and the whole film can be considered a parable. In many ways, the protagonist reminds us of Jesus Christ, and not only because of his long hair and beard. Keoma, like Jesus, was reviled by his "brothers" (Jewish religious extremists), but protected and helped by his father. So, the members of Caldwell's band would be equivalent to something like the Pharisees. Jesus Christ was also a "half-breed": half divine, half human. Keoma seeks redemption for his people, and he too ends up being "crucified"; on a wheel. This western is not as full of allegories as "El Topo" (Alejandro Jodorowsky, 1970), but we see that it can have various interpretations, and that surely there is a deep meaning.

The script was written by Luigi Montefiori, better known as George Eastman - who would stand out as an actor in the

134

excellent "Rabid dogs" (Mario Bava, 1974) and in "Antropophagus" (Joe D'Amato, 1980).

Director Enzo G. Castellari considers "Keoma" to be one of his best films. His polizziesco "The big racket", shot in the same year in 1976, is also highly praiseworthy. A sequel to "Keoma" is announced for 2017, which will also be directed by Castellari and will feature Franco Nero in the leading role.

The soundtrack was composed by the brothers Guido and Maurizio De Angelis. Both would form the duo "Oliver Onions" and would be in charge of the musical accompaniment of series from our childhood such as "D´Artacán y los tres mosqueperros"("Dogtanian and the three muskehounds") or "La vuelta al mundo de Willy Fog" (Around the world with Willy Fog) (from 1981 and 1983, respectively).

George is played by Woody Strode, who has a secondary role at the beginning of "Once upon a time in the West" (Sergio Leone, 1968) and whom we also saw in "The Italian Connection" (1972) and in "Loaded guns" (1975), both by Fernando Di Leo.

Orso Maria Guerrini plays Butch, one of Keoma's brothers. This actor would participate almost a couple of decades later in the saga of "La Piovra", specifically in the fifth and season.

William Berger (who plays the father) and Donald O'Brien (Caldwell) take part in the aforementioned "Mannaja", filmed the following year by Sergio Martino.

Mannaja (a.k.a. "A man called Blade")

Italy, 1977

Filmaker: Sergio Martino

Script: Sergio Martino, Sauro Scavolini

Cast: Maurizio Merli (Mannaja), John Steiner (Valler), Sonja Jeannine (Deborah), Donald O'Brien (Burt Craven)

Music: Guido De Angelis, Maurizio De Angelis

Plot

Bounty hunter Mannaja is not only an expert with a revolver; he is also very skilled in handling a small axe that he always carries with him and uses as a throwing weapon. Mannaja chases a wanted criminal through the overcast and swampy countryside. When he finally catches him, he takes him to the nearest town with the intention of handing him over to the local sheriff and collecting the money offered for his head.

But that town, to which Mannaja and the man he arrested for him arrive in the middle of a storm, has no sheriff. The laws there are regulated by a powerful mining magnate named McGowan. His company mercilessly exploits the locals, who work like slaves in his silver mines.

In the town hall, Mannaja has his first meeting with Valler, McGowan's right-hand man. Valler is the leader of a large group of gunmen who control the miners. Initially, Mannaja's only intention is to hand over the fugitive and collect the reward. Since Valler is not willing to pay him a penny for his prey, Mannaja challenges McGowan's lieutenant to a card game: $5,000 will be the amount bet. When Valler insists on seeing his opponent's $5,000, he points to his detainee and shows him the "wanted" sign, which states that this is the money to be paid to whoever delivers him. Valler only accepts because he is convinced that he will win thanks to his tricks. But to his amazement Mannaja wins the game, and he gets the money. The perplexed Valler orders his henchmen to shoot at the bounty hunter, but the latter reacts quickly and shoots at the hands of the gunmen. He then leaves the saloon with $5,000 and his captive. Valler will not forget such an outrage...

Seeing McGowan's name written in several places in the village, Mannaja has some flashbacks... The mining entrepreneur seems to be somehow related to his past.

Since he has already obtained the money he wanted and has no one to give the criminal, that same night Mannaja decides to release him. The next morning, he goes to the mines to watch the locals being exploited by Valler and his henchmen. Mannaja watches the silver being loaded onto a horse-drawn carriage, which he follows at a safe distance. He is not too surprised when, a few miles away, the carriage is attacked by bandits... The outlaws are part of the team of gunmen in the service of Valler. In this way, the bounty hunter with the axe proves that McGowan's right arm not only enslaves the local men, but is also disloyal to his boss, plundering the silver from the mines he owns.

Mannaja enters McGowan's residence, meeting first with his daughter Debra and soon after with the tycoon; a paralyzed man in a wheelchair. Moments later, Valler appears as well. A new fight takes place between him and the bounty hunter, who manages to humiliate his opponent once again...

When Mannaja is about to leave the village, he is the victim of an attack ordered by Valler: They have dynamited some steep slopes so that large rocks fall on the bounty hunter. Mannaja is presumed dead, but in reality he has only been wounded. Later, he is found by the dancers of a theatre company who were going with their director in a caravan to a new city to perform. The girls will take him with them and especially one of them, Angela, will look after him until he recovers. Mannaja and the young woman will fall in love.

Meanwhile, the perfidious Valler carries out with his bandits the kidnapping of Debra, McGowan's daughter, while he was supposed to escort the girl on a stage...

Commentary

"Mannaja"/"A Man called Blade" is in my opinion one of the best Western films ever made, along with Leone's, Corbucci's "Django" (1966) and Giulio Questi's atypical "Oro Maldito" (1967).

This is a violent twilight Italo-Western (shot when the genre was no longer in fashion) directed and written by Sergio Martino - a leading exponent of bloody horror, the polizziesco and the giallo (his titles include "The suspicious death of a minor", 1975; "The case of the scorpion´s tale", 1971; or "Torso", 1973).

138

It is possible to find some narrative parallels with the work of his brilliant namesake Sergio Leone, especially with "Once upon a time in America" (1968). Just as in that film the protagonist "Harmonica" (Charles Bronson) acts motivated by an old desire for revenge that is not fully revealed until the end, Mannaja also has a score to settle for decades with one of the villains he must face. And just as in Leone's epic western the locomotive magnate is a crippled man whom his henchman Frank aims to displace, in Martino's proposal the paralysed businessman McGowan will be betrayed by his ambitious employee Valler.

Among the original contributions of "Mannaja" (in addition to the main character's predilection for the throwing axe) we find elements that approach horror films: a supernatural and gloomy aura envelops the entire film from the beginning. The oppressive atmosphere is very well taken care of.

One of the most memorable scenes is the assault on the stage to kidnap Debra, with the consequent execution of her fellow travelers; murdered in cold blood - these brutal sequences are interspersed with the cheerful performance of the can-can dancers in the neighboring town. The cameramen and editors do a splendid job here.

The film features unpredictable twists in the script, increasing dramatic tension, unexpected betrayals and a subtle critique of the greed of the then nascent exploitative capitalism so characteristic of the "Protestant ethic" that was taking hold in the mid-19th century in the Old West. The tone of the film is extremely pessimistic and apocalyptic.

The actor Maurizio Merli, who gives life to the main bounty hunter, is famous in Italy above all for having taken part, always in the role of a tough curator, in innumerable polizzieschi - among them "Violent Naples" or "The tough ones", both by Umberto Lenzi and from 1976.

The soundtrack, which features a song in English about the hero of the axe ("He, alone, a solitary man..."), was composed by the De Angelis brothers.

He killed him like a dog but he still laughed... (O.V. Lo ammazzò come un cane... ma lui rideva ancora)

Italy, 1972

Director: Angelo "Elo" Pannacciò (as Mark Welles)

Script: Elo Pannaciò, Craig Marina

Cast: Michael Forest (Nick Barton), Giuseppe Cardillo (Kimble), Susanna Levi (Suzy Barton), Antonio Molino Rojo (Ramson

Music: Daniele Patucchi

Plot

A group of outlaws assaults Barton's ranch at night, killing the old owner and raping the women. Kimble, one of the bandits, takes no part in the atrocities, believing they were only going to steal the horses. Soon after, he decides to abandon his cronies, because he does not approve of their ferocious methods.

When Ramson, the gang's leader, is informed that Kimble is leaving the group, he takes it as a desertion. Besides, Kimble knows too much, and he might run off with the sheriff. So, Ramson orders his wayward subordinate liquidated.

Meanwhile, Nick Barton returns to his family's ranch and finds a hellish scenario: a massacre from which only his sister (?) Jane survived. The young woman has been raped and is badly injured, but she manages to recover. Nick swears revenge on the graves of his relatives.

Nick Barton begins to ride in search of the killers. He only knows about them the few things Jane could tell him: That there were five of them, and that they went in that direction. Anxious to settle their accounts, Nick asks a man on the road if he has seen them pass by. The man questioned, playing a flute he always wears around his neck, is none other than Kimble.

Kimble sets out to help Nick find the fugitives - hiding the fact that he was part of the gang himself, and that he was present when the massacre against his family was committed. In exchange for a certain amount of money, Kimble offers to take him to "the four". But Nick knows, from what his sister told him, that there were actually five...

Both will look for the bandits, while the bandits also try to find Kimble to kill him; they consider him an uncomfortable witness. When Ramson and his henchmen learn that Jane survived the assault, they decide that the girl must also be eliminated...

Commentary

Low-budget Western, with an interesting but not too original approach. A very similar story is the narrative thread of "Da uomo a uomo" (Giulio Petroni, 1967), starring Lee Van Cleef and John Phillip Law. On that occasion, a young man eager to avenge his family joins a veteran gunman in hunting down the killers of his parents and sister... unaware that his ally was part of that gang.

Something very similar happens on this occasion, although without the epic tone of Petroni's film - which has clearly "Leonese" reminiscences.

The director of the film is Angelo "Elo" Panacciò, who made his debut here behind the scenes under the pseudonym of "Mark Welles". This director was responsible for "Sex of the Witch" (1973), a sort of crossover between giallo and gothic horror with multiple erotic-softcore elements; a common feature of his not very prolific filmography. In addition to a rip-off of "The Exorcist" ("Un urlo dalle tenebre" / "A Cry from the Darkness", 1975), Panacciò later directed another Western film (even more unknown and forgotten) with the bizarre title of "Porno Erotico Western" (1979).

The name of this feature film, "He killed him like a dog but he still laughed...", is probably the most interesting part of it (and in that title there is certainly the key of the end of the film...). The soundtrack in many aspects reminds more of a melodrama than of the Italian-Western. It was composed by Daniele Patucchi, author of the music of the memorable but misunderstood "Frankenstein'80" (Mario Mancini, 1972).

Ramson, the gang's leader, is played by the Spaniard Antonio Molino Rojo; a regular secondary actor of the sub-genre, who participates among other titles in "The Good, the Bad and the Ugly" (Sergio Leone, 1966).

Get mean

Italy, 1975

Director: Ferdinando Baldi

Script: Wolfe Lowenthal, Lloyd Battista (based on Tony Anthony's story)

Cast: Tony Anthony (Stranger), Lloyd Battista (Shadow), Raf Baldassarre (Diego), Diana Lorys (Princess Elisabeth María de Burgos), Mirta Miller (Morelia)

Music: Franco Bixio, Fabio Frizzi, Vince Tempera

Plot

In an arid village in the west, a newcomer is hired by the few remaining inhabitants to carry out a dangerous task: he must escort Princess Elisabeth María de Burgos to Spain, so that she can claim her rightful right to the throne. An army of barbarians commanded by don Diego will try to prevent it.

After a long journey on horseback and having crossed the ocean by boat, the stranger and the princess arrive in Spain. There they find themselves in the middle of a battle between the barbarians and the Moors. The former are victorious and capture the princess. The stranger is hung upside down, but soon after that a young girl named María arrives. She and her friends free him so that the gunman can help them against the barbarian oppressors. The stranger wants to rescue the princess, fulfill his mission and collect the $50,000 he was promised. When he learns of the existence of Don Rodrigo's legendary treasure, he will also try to get it...

Commentary

An unusual and unclassifiable product, which in the context of western film combines genres such as sword and sorcery with horror - all full of anachronisms and with touches of surrealist comedy in the style of Monty Python. Although the theme is not very original (the main character's mission is to protect a princess and find a treasure), the approach and context in which the story takes place is very original indeed: From the Wild West we go to (medieval?) Spain; in the same film we have a gunman who, armed with his colt, has to face a horde of barbarian warriors with huge swords and horned helmets; likewise, María's companions seem to have come out of a chapter of "Curro Jiménez"(Spanish TV series from the late ´70s, about a Robin-Hood-like bandit), dressed in the style of the Andalusian bandits of the early 19th century.

Later, to access the treasure, one must pass a kind of initiation test (follow "the footprints of death"), entering a sinister crypt full of skeletons. Numerous intrigues will follow one another.

The nameless stranger who is the protagonist is not necessarily a hero; during the battle between the barbarians and the Moors he considers that the best thing is to escape, and little by little we will see that he not only lacks courage but also scruples, since the only thing he is interested in is getting his hands on the money.

Amorality is a common trait in the main characters of Italian-style westerns (they are usually bounty hunters, for example); but that's the only thing this film has in common with the subgenre inaugurated by the great Sergio Leone. That, and the fact that the main character has no name (as Clint Eastwood didn't have one in the famous Dollar Trilogy). However, this strange movie is far more loquacious than most italo-westerns, and he doesn't stop making supposedly funny comments. As far as the princess is concerned, she is an arrogant woman (according to her status) and somewhat neurotic - which on more than one occasion will drive her "bodyguard" crazy.

The stranger is played by Tony Anthony, who also is behind the original idea for the script and produced the feature film. This actor was also involved in two other unusual westerns: in one of them, "The silent stranger" (Luigi Vanzi, 1968) he plays a gunman who goes on a diplomatic mission to Japan, where he must mediate in a dispute between samurai clans (I won't tire of mentioning the countless parallels between the Japanese chanbara and the western genre, particularly in its Italian variant). In the other film, Anthony gives life to a blind gunman in "Blindman" (Ferdinando Baldi, 1971) - this Baldi is certainly also the director of the film in question. The idea of a blind gunman was certainly "borrowed" from the Japanese films of "Zatoichi" (the wandering blind swordsman, played by Shintaro

Katsu, and about whom a whole series of films was made between the 60s and 80s). In "Blindman", the Beatle Ringo Starr participates as an actor.

The soundtrack, composed among others by Fabio Frizzi - who would later become Lucio Fulci's recurrent musical collaborator ("City of the living dead", "The Beyond", "Zombi 2"...) - deserves to be highlighted.

Annex:

El Topo

Mexico, 1970

Director: Alejandro Jodorowsky

Script: Alejandro Jodorowsky

Cast: Alejandro Jodorowsky (El Topo), Brontis Jodorowsky (Son of el Topo), Alfonso Arau (Bandit 1), Mara Lorenzio (Mara), Paula Romo (Stranger), Jacqueline Luis (Little Woman), Robert John (Son of el Topo, adult)

Music: Alejandro Jodorowsky

Plot

A gunman dressed in black leather crosses the desert with his young son. The mysterious individual, known as "El Topo" ("The Mole"), makes the completely naked child bury a cuddly toy and a photograph of a woman in the sand: "You are now seven years old and already a man. Bury your first toy and your mother's picture".

Father and son continue on the back of their horse until they reach an abandoned village where a massacre has taken place. Puddles of blood everywhere, rotting corpses, gutted animals... A multitude of hanged men hang inside a ransacked church.

A dying man is found and the mole asks who committed the atrocious carnage. The dying man begs him to kill him, for he cannot bear the suffering. Topo hands the gun to his son, who fires the kill shot. After that, he puts some extravagant rings on his fingers.

Not far from there, a group of fetishistic Mexican bandits have their hideout. One delights in caressing some women's shoes (which he then shoots with his revolver to practice his aim), another cuts a banana into slices with his sabre and then eats the pieces, and the third outlines on the rocky ground the figure of a woman using little stones and then lies on top of her in a coital attitude...

The bandits see the Mole arrive and go out to meet him with burlesque merriment. Near them is a flock of bleating sheep. One of the outlaws inflates a balloon, which he places on the ground. The air is coming out of a tiny hole, and everyone understands that when the balloon deflates it will be time to draw and fire. The Mole is the fastest and eliminates two of his opponents. The third, who was in the middle, is disarmed, wounded and questioned about where the rest of the gang and their leader are. When he receives the information he needs, the Mole finishes off the outlaw and puts his rings in the dead man's mouth.

The other bandits have barricaded themselves in a convent, where they are holding the friars hostage. The religious men are subjected to fierce mockery: they must witness how one of the evildoers blows his nose with the pages he tears out of a Bible. Then the criminals put on music on a record player and start dancing with the young monks in a clearly homosexual attitude. These bandits are even more depraved and savage than the previous ones. They are completely deranged and enjoy spreading terror. Their leader, the Colonel, is an individual who resides inside a stone tower with a slave girl. Initially he wears only red underwear and is bald, but with the help of his maid he puts on a toupee and dresses in a pompous uniform reminiscent of Napoleon. The woman goes outside and is immediately harassed by the rampaging bandits. But they pale and become meek and docile when the Colonel appears in all his majesty. Behind him, a herd of pigs emerges from the tower. In the presence of the Colonel (who represents the authority) the bloodthirsty outlaws behave exaggeratedly submissive.

El Topo arrives with his son and disarms the stunned criminals without them putting up much resistance. After that, the vigilante challenges the Colonel to a duel and defeats him by humiliating him before his vassals: with one shot he blows his toupee off. His ostentatious uniform is torn to shreds. The beastly bandits, who until now had venerated their leader doggedly, now turn against him; they beat him and shake him frantically laughing. El Topo castrates the Colonel to the great delight of those present. The Authority has been destroyed, the gang dissolved, and the overthrown leader commits suicide by shooting himself in the mouth.

The Colonel's slave girl falls madly in love with El Topo after his heroic deed. The avenging gunman decides to abandon his son to the friars and take instead the woman he has freed from the clutches of the gang.

El Topo and his woman, whom the mysterious vigilante will call Mara, now set out on a long journey through the desert.

In order to survive in these torrid places, el Topo performs several miracles: he shoots a rock and a stream of water begins to flow from it, or he finds eggs buried under the sand. Mara tries, too, but she is incapable of such feats. After the Mole has possessed her with a bestial fury, Mara proposes to the gunman a "test of love": Find the "Four Masters of the Revolver" hidden in the desert, face them in duels and kill them. To find them, they must always "walk in a spiral".

After many months they find the first master: a squalid young blind guru with effeminate features (despite his moustache) who resides in a stone tower in the middle of the desert next to two crippled servants; one without legs and the other without arms (the latter always carries the first one on his back). In the kind of mound where he receives el Topo there is a sheep.

El Topo laments with Mara, fearing that he will be unable to kill him, but she encourages him and tells him that she wants him to be victorious at any price. So they both set up a trap to kill the guru in a treacherous way...

After assassinating the first Master of the Revolver, a mysterious Amazon (dressed in black like el Topo) proposes to take them to the second one. The latter, a chubby and hairy individual dressed as a Cossack, lives with his mother, "speaks" telepathically and is dedicated to making fragile but complex geometric figures. Neither does el Topo kill the Second Master in a clean duel, but with treacherous methods; from the back and by surprise.

150

After this, el Topo and the two women continue the march "towards the centre", "in a spiral", until they reach the Third Master; who lives in a place full of rabbits. This guru perceives that el Topo will be a disloyal opponent, because from the moment the gunman enters his enclosure, his rabbits all begin to die. The two face off in a duel with guns loaded with a single bullet. The master is faster and the bullet hits el Topo's chest. But the Mole had placed a small metal plate at heart level. Now he shoots, killing the third master.

Only the last one remains to be killed. The fourth is an old man with a butterfly net that challenges el Topo to a close combat. The gunman tries to hit him, but the Old Man always quickly dodges his punches. When el Topo is exhausted, the fourth master says "you can never kill me" and shoots himself, killing himself. Thus preventing the Mole from completing his mission. El Topo has been unable to kill the Four Masters as he had promised to Mara. The gunman despairs and sinks into an abyss of delirium (among other things he sees the sheep of the first master crucified in his collapsing stone tower).

The mysterious woman who accompanied Mara and him is determined to replace him after his flagrant defeat. The horsewoman in black unlocks several shots at him as they meet on a long, narrow bridge. When el Topo is badly wounded, the mysterious woman gives Mara her gun and tells her to choose: "Either him or me". Mara, disappointed with her man, shoots at el Topo. He falls down and the two women leave together on horseback.

Many years later, el Topo wakes up in a grotto with a beard and graying hair. He "resurrected" after a long catatonic trance. A female dwarf has been looking after him all that time. There resides a colony of beings that are deformed "after years of incest", as the dwarf explains. She also tells him that her people are trapped inside the mountain, the outside world can only be accessed through a small hole at the top.

El Topo is brought before an old shaman who eats giant beetles, and gives them to him to try (they probably have entheogenic properties). A "second birth" of el Topo occurs, ritualistic and symbolic. The dwarf girl shaves his head and beard; now the old gunman is a new man, with a humble robe and the appearance of a Buddhist monk.

The Mole now sets out to free the cripples from their captivity inside the cave, so that they can live in the nearby village.

However, the residents of that village are as wicked, cruel and heartless as the Mexican bandits (albeit with a hypocritical mask of respectability). A cult has taken control of the village, and the symbol of it is present everywhere: An eye locked inside an equilateral triangle.

In order for the deformed ones to surface, el Topo and his new friend will have to dig a tunnel that connects the cave to the outside world. Thus, both emerge through the small hole at the top of the mountain and head for the village, intending to beg for the necessary money to buy shovels, picks and dynamite.

Soon the dwarf is disenchanted by the evil atmosphere in that village: "Do you think it's worth it for my people to leave the cave and come here?"

However, both of them get down to work: They put on little street clown shows, clean toilets, and with the money they earn they buy the tools to dig the tunnel...

One day a young Franciscan friar with a beard and long hair arrives in the village. He has a certain similarity to the Mole in his time as a gunman... For he is his son: the naked boy el Topo abandoned many years ago with the monks in the convent...

Commentary

Alejandro Jodorowsky's "El Topo" is anything but a conventional movie.
The multifaceted Chilean Jewish artist and "psychomagician" who has lived in France for years wrote, directed, starred in and composed the music for this very personal first film of his (he had previously directed "Fando y Lis", but that film was based on a play of the same name by his friend Fernando Arrabal). Producers of "El Topo" were Moshe Rosemberg and Roberto Viskin. Also Juan López Moctezuma, Mexican director of B series horror films (like "Alucarda"), partially financed the project.

Filmed and released in Mexico, "El Topo" did not receive a very warm welcome in that country. But when the film was screened in New York as part of a late-night movie session (which would kick off "Midnight Movies") it quickly became a real sensation, a "cult film" in the context of the counterculture of the early 1970s, an iconic and "visionary" film that would delight the hippie crowd - John Lennon declared "El Topo" to be one of his favorite films.

This is a bizarre cocktail of "new age" pseudo-spirituality that combines biblical messianism, a hint of Zen Buddhism degraded to the merely picturesque, and large doses of Buñuelian surrealism - all drinking from the stylistic influences of the Italian-style western. More important than the plot or the narrative aspect is the rich visual power of the film, full of dreamlike, absurd and sublimely chaotic scenes and situations (as in a dream... or a nightmare). To paraphrase the director, "El Topo is not a comedy, a tragedy, a political or religious film; it is all of these at the same time" - and can be subjected to multiple interpretations.

The film's prologue tells us that "The mole is an animal that digs underground tunnels. When it goes outside and sees the sun, it becomes blind". Hence the appropriate nickname of the protagonist, who in the first part is a gunman in constant search of redemption and enlightenment; and who in the second part (transformed into a humble mendicant monk) literally digs a tunnel (so that the introductory phrase makes even more sense).

"El Topo" has scenes of great violence, with a bloody and Dantesque imagery. There are also extremely disturbing moments, such as the homoerotic sordidness of the bandits who try to abuse the young friars, or the scene in which the seven-year-old boy (completely naked except for a hat to protect him from the sun) is abandoned by his father in the convent and the friars surround him with implicit intentions - The boy is played by Brontis Jodorowsky, one of the director's sons in real life.

The mysticism that permeates the film is clearly "new age", arbitrarily mixing religions and spiritual paths: a Zen Buddhism of "walking around" that was very fashionable in the West in those years ("I let bullets go through the emptiness of my heart", "I am not afraid to kill you because death does not exist"...). Also the famous koan that says "If you meet Buddha on the way...kill him!" is taken by Jodorowsky to the big screen in the first part of his film (where he dedicates himself to murdering the Four Masters, always using dirty tricks - something that Mara, his archetypal temptress "Eva", has pushed him into. By the way, "Mara" is also the name of a demon who tried to prevent Siddhartha Gautama, the Buddha, from reaching enlightenment).

In his stage as an avenging gunman, el Topo has a certain yahvitic old-testamentarian character: He is a "vigilante" of "an eye for an eye and a tooth for a tooth", who annihilates everybody who rivals him in the ostentation of power (the Colonel, who represents authority and the established order, asks him "Who are you?", el Topo answers: "I am God!") When el Topo and his woman are wandering in the desert (as "the chosen people"), the gunman performs some "miracles" comparable to those of Moses.

Later, in the village, the fanatical cult that has settled there has obvious demiurgic connotations: with the "all-seeing eye", transformed into the sacred symbol that has replaced the cross (later, the son of the Mole, a "monk-soldier", will tear off that blasphemous and usurper emblem that also covered the walls inside the church).

The scene of the "Russian roulette" inside the church is memorable in the highest degree: The parish priest passes a revolver to the parishioners, while everyone sings in ecstasy "You are protecting us, Lord!" (with a rhythmic cadence reminiscent of a mantra). Several volunteer, and pointing one after the other at their respective temples, they pull the trigger... It's a trick, because there is no real bullet. But the son of el Topoe, who is present, puts a real bullet into the drum of the gun, and a child blows his brains out...

The film is clearly structured in two parts: The first one, in which the Mole is a wandering gunman and the second one, after his magical "resurrection" in the depth of the cave; when he emerges characterized as a kind of Buddhist monk (Some have established the biblical parallelism according to which the first part would represent the Old Testament and the second one the New). But the film could also be considered to be divided into three segments: The first until the Mole defeats the Colonel, the second since he abandons his son for Mara and crosses the desert "in a spiral" with her in order to kill the "Four Masters", and the third from his symbolic resurrection onwards: With his new companion the dwarf in the perverse town dominated by the fanatical sect.

Each Master that the Mole has to face is always more powerful than the previous one, although at the same time he has less material possessions. The first one owns a stone tower, has two slaves at his service and two guns. The second lives in a kind of wagon with his mother and has a revolver. The third lives in an open-air enclosure with the only company of some rabbits, and his gun is loaded with a single bullet. And the fourth and last is an old man who is not even armed (but who manages to defeat the Mole by killing himself, thus preventing the gunman from fulfilling his objective).

The film does not involve professional actors or people who are used to working in front of the cameras (with the exception of Jodorowsky himself). His first partner, Mara, is played by a young woman whose name was also Mara in real life. Jodorowsky hosted her in his home in Mexico City after finding her in a state of psychosis caused by LSD abuse. Jodorowsky met the gunwoman in black (the female counterpart of el Topo) in a strip club. Paula Romo worked there as a dancer. Neither of them ever participated in any film production again (Worthy of mention, by the way, is the allegorically erotic scene of the mysterious Amazon cracking the prickly pear in the desert).

In spite of its questionable counter-initiative intentions (promoting a "new age" esotericism; that is, banalized, desacralized and adulterated) "El Topo" is a very interesting film at all levels. Of great artistic quality and enormous visual impact, its atmosphere is very well achieved. Also very effective is the music that accompanies the film, which includes guttural Tibetan mantra songs during the duels. The soundtrack highlights the unreal and dreamlike character of the story. It would be interesting to know if Dalí, Buñuel or Sergio Leone came to see the film and what they thought of it.

El tunco Maclovio ("One-armed Maclovio") (a.k.a. "Deuda de muerte", i.e. "Deadly Debt")

Mexico, 1970

Director: Alberto Mariscal

Script: José Delfos

Cast: Julio Alemán (Maclovio), Juan Miranda (Julián), Mario Almada (Juan Mariscal), Barbara Angely (Sara Montaño), Eric del Castillo (Yuma), Carlos Agostí (Curator)

Music: Ernesto Cortázar

Plot

Laura Montaño, a landowner and rancher somewhere in northern Mexico, sends an emissary in search of Maclovio Castro, a lone gunman and contract killer, better known as "el tunco" ("the one-armed man"). The messenger, who has drunk poisoned water along the way, writhes in pain and asks Maclovio to end his suffering. Undaunted, the gunman shoots him in the head and heads for Laura Montaño's ranch (that's how forceful the filmic preamble is, after which the credits begin).

The powerful lady has numerous enemies in the region, and intends to hire the "tunco" to eliminate them. The ranchera has gradually taken control of the other ranches, plunging entire families into misery. Although she has a detachment of ruthless henchmen at her service, none of them have the gun skills attributed to the legendary Maclovio.

One of the ranchers whose land was expropriated by the hacienda has a son who is in love with Laura Montaño's daughter Sara. The father, surnamed Moncada, knows that the tunco Maclovio has been hired to kill his son. For his part, a sheriff is also aware of the arrival of the famous hitman in the region, and intends to hunt him down (since he also has a personal account pending with him).

Shortly before arriving at Laura Montaño's property, the tunco is assaulted by a ragged young man, who points a shotgun at him and asks for food. The boy, an orphan who introduces himself as Marcelo, is one of the victims of the poverty that plagues the region. The two become friends and the young man offers himself as his assistant.

Chased by the sheriff and his men, Maclovio heads for a narrow gorge. There, on the edge of an abyss, he meets Julián Moncada, coincidentally the man he must liquidate...

When Sara learns that her mother has hired Maclovio to kill Julian, she begins to think of ways to eliminate the mysterious gunman. To do so, she will try to use Yuma, the most ferocious of the henchmen on her ranch, and like Julián, her suitor.

Commentary

If Sergio Corbucci presents us with a mute gunman with his "Il grande Silenzio" (1968), in this Mexican western we have one who is one-armed (for that is what the word "tunco" means in some areas of Latin America), thus contributing to the Western cinema to the variant that has as protagonists lonely and enigmatic gunmen with physical defects - Another example would be the "Blindman" by Ferdinando Baldi (1971), more than probably inspired by the jidaigeki saga of the blind Zatoichi.

This film helped launch two well-known Mexican actors to stardom: Julio Alemán (who plays the leading role of Tunco Maclovio) and Mario Almada (who plays the sheriff Juan Mariscal), and who we have already seen in interesting films such as the thriller "Cazador de asesinos"("Hunter of killers") (José Luis Urquieta, 1983) or the atypical western with supernatural touches "El extraño hijo del sheriff" ("The strange son of the sheriff") (Fernado Durán Rojas, 1982). Almada also has a minor role in the memorable and underrated "Violación" (Valentín Trujillo, 1989). Recently deceased at age 94, veteran Mario Almada was participating in films right up to the end; and over the past two decades he took part in a large number of "narco-films" (an action-packed, low-budget subgenre of crime movies, usually set in northern Mexico in the context of drug-cartel fights; and which curiously shares many characteristics with the western genre).

Returning to "El Tunco Maclovio", this is a film with a powerful dramatic charge, extremely tragic and quite pessimistic, which manages to explore with great success the deep character of the characters. Explicit violence abounds, and director Mariscal is obviously inspired by the aesthetics and canons of the Italian-style western (El Tunco, a lonely, hieratic man of few words, is reminiscent of the Clint Eastwood of the Leonian Dollar Trilogy). By the way, the Italian title of this Mexican production was "Viveva per uccidere, uccideva per vivere" - which translates as "He lived to kill, he killed to live".

Santo contra los jinetes del terror (Santo vs. the Terror Riders)

Mexico, 1970

Director: René Cardona

Script: René Cardona, Jesús "Murciélago" Velázquez

Cast: El Santo, Armando Silvestre, Julio Aldama, Mary Montiel

Music: Gustavo César Carrión

Plot

Six inmates escape from a leper colony one night, in the surroundings of a remote village in an arid region of northern Mexico. Panic soon sets in among the locals. Everyone fears contagion, the spread of an epidemic. In addition, lepers break into some houses to steal food. Sheriff Darío tries to keep the situation under control. But tempers are running high among the villagers. One of them, the tough Camerino, insists that the lepers must be killed. But Darío believes that compassion must be shown to them, they are sick people who are not to blame for their situation; they must be captured by using cunning to return them to the leper colony.

The local authorities order that the houses that were raided by the lepers be burned down, to prevent the spread of the plague. This almost causes a rebellion among the villagers. The popular anger is capitalized on by Camerino. Both he and the sheriff organize groups of volunteers to go hunting for the leper.

One night, an outlaw with his face covered enters Carmen's house with the intention of stealing. The girl is Darío's girlfriend, and she lives with her elderly father. When he is discovered by the old man, the bandit shoots, killing him. Carmen is convinced that the criminal is one of the escaped lepers. She and the rest of the village put pressure on Darío to finish them off as soon as possible.

Meanwhile, the outlaw who has shot Carmen's father meets up with his accomplices in a cantina: It turns out to be Camerino, who intentionally intended to blame the lepers for his misdeeds. Now that the lepers are in the surroundings, he wants to take advantage of the situation to carry out a series of coups for which everyone would hold the deformed fugitives responsible.

And not only that: Camerino also wants to "form a partnership" with the lepers. He goes looking for them in the "Devil's Cave" where they have been hiding and proposes that they become part of his gang ("The world has too much, we have too little and you have nothing"). José, chief and spokesman for the lepers, accepts. But he ignores that the perfidious Camerino only intends to use them as cannon fodder. The leader of the bandits talks of sharing with them fifty percent of what they steal, when in reality he intends to treacherously liquidate them after they have committed the coups, when they are no longer useful.

Overwhelmed by the crime wave and the panic of the locals, Darío decides to call the Saint, "defender of justice and protector of the helpless".

Santo arrives at the village galloping on the back of a horse, and immediately starts to work to restore order. One of the first things he does is talk to the director of the leper colony, to find out about the characteristics of the disease. The expert confirms that the movements of those affected are always "clumsy and lacking in agility" – which contrasts with the way in which, according to many witnesses, several of the criminals were moving. This arouses the suspicions of Santo, who intuits that it is not only lepers who devote themselves to looting and murdering.

Commentary

Without a doubt, one of the most interesting and original (as well as unknown) films among the fifty-or-so in which the famous "Enmascarado de Plata" participated. As far as I know, this is the only incursion of Santo into the western genre. The fusion between western and wrestling genres results in an extremely enjoyable film.

We don't know for sure when the story develops (westerns are usually set in the second half of the 19th century, and the Saint's films are usually set contemporary to the time they were filmed). But the truth is that this is not important, since we are dealing with a timeless film jewel; not only a crossover of genres but also, apparently, one of periods takes place.

The lepers play a role analogous to that of the zombies, which were in vogue at the time after the success of "The Night of the Living Dead" (George Romero, 1968). Both in their appearance and in the way they move and the reactions provoked by the six escaped lepers remind us of those putrid walking corpses (also in the fact that whoever gets too close to them will suffer the inevitable contagion) – the difference is that lepers have a conscience, and in fact consider themselves dead in life. They no longer have anything to lose, and have escaped to die "in the open". The villagers see them as terrible monsters, but they do not see that those who manipulate and use them are even worse. Only Santo, who besides being a great fighter is very sagacious, understands that someone very Machiavellian is behind the crimes; the lepers only have the role of disposable pawns.

When Santo arrives in the village, Camerino challenges him: In front of everyone he tries to ridicule him, saying that if he is a real man he does not need a mask, and that if he wears one it may be because he is one of the lepers... Then there is a hand-to-hand combat between the vigilante and the braggart, in which the second one will take the loss. Thus, the animosity of Camerino towards the Saint grows, and the hero will have to walk cautiously because of the machinations of the bandit.

We also see a fight in which the winner can get a few thousand pesos. Santo intervenes spontaneously with the intention of donating the prize to an orphanage. The nuns who run the institution cheer him on in a rage.

In addition to the relationship between Carmen (Mary Montiel) and Sheriff Damián (Julio Aldama), we see the bitter and truncated love between José, the head of the lepers, and his girlfriend Lupe (whom he has not seen since his illness began). He is only looking for her to "say goodbye" to her, since he knows that they will never be able to be together again in this life... (Or maybe they will, thanks to the Saint's help?)

We have almost everything in this film by the great René Cardona: an intelligent and subtle early zombie-exploitation (the wave of zombie films would arrive a decade later from Italy), where the lepers act as the living dead; drama, intrigue, adventure, comedy, love and explicit violence (the murders are quite graphic), all in a western context (Italian style) and with the protagonism of the masked wrestler par excellence: the invincible Santo.

As for the technical aspect, the abundant use of camera sweeping between sequences is striking.

The idea for the screenplay (which he wrote in collaboration with Cardona) came from Jesús "Murciélago" ("Bat") Velázquez; another Mexican wrestler who, in addition to handing out blows in the ring and sporadically intervening as an actor, was also a writer.

Burn, baby, burn (a.k.a. "Dead aim", a.k.a. "Rattlesnake", a.k.a. "Lucky Johnny")

Mexico/Italy, 1971-1975

Director: José Antonio Bolaños

Script: José Bolaños, Pedro F. Miret, Tony Monaco

Cast: Glen Lee (Johnny), Venetia Vianello (Kelly), James Westerfield (John Applebee), Carlos East (Deek), Jorge Russek (Curator)

Music: Luchi De Jesus

Plot

A man realizes that his wife has left him for her lover, taking with her their small child. He tries to catch up with them in the desert and a gun battle ensues, in which all but the child die. The child, about two years old, crawls in the desert and a rattlesnake approaches him threateningly. But an individual dressed in black appears to help him. He kills the snake, cuts off its rattle and gives it to little Johnny as a toy. The stranger is the gravedigger John Applebee, who adopts the now orphaned boy.

The years go by and Johnny is an adult. He and his adoptive father travel through the villages of the wild west, plying their deadly trade. These are the years of the civil war between the South and the North. Still, it seems that there is not much work, so Applebee and Johnny devote themselves to make sure that they do not lack orders... Killing people so that they can be paid for their burials. They also appropriate the valuables of their "customers": They strip the bodies of any money they may have on them, as well as their boots and their guns. They even keep their clothes. They are real human vultures.

Johnny was very young when he lost his parents, but his encounter with the rattlesnake was burned into his childish mind shortly before he was picked up by Applebee. Thus, every time he hears the whistle and the characteristic sound of that reptile, he is possessed by a kind of trance.

The gravedigger has taught him how to handle firearms. They both ride from place to place performing their sinister task. But they are tired of that lifestyle, of always wandering around the desert aimlessly, and of living off the few dollars they get from their prey. Johnny proposes to the old man to rob a bank. That way they would get a large amount of money that they could invest in a funeral business to live the rest of their days peacefully. But Applebee doesn't seem too keen on the idea.

One day, Johnny sees a couple arguing in an oasis. It's Maria, a saloon dancer, and Jack, an expert gambler. The two of them are planning to hold up a gold stage. Informed of their plans, Johnny resolves to go ahead of them...

Commentary

A curious and unknown western co-production between Mexico and Italy, shot in 1971 but not released until 1974.

The premise of the plot is quite interesting, but throughout the film there are numerous inconsistencies resulting in a final product that is quite confusing. The soundtrack is also quite irregular. Good sound effects (which in a way remind us of the also atypical western "Mátalo!" by Cesare Canevari) and funky rhythms typical of the time of filming; but in some moments the scenes are accompanied by a melodramatic music out of place.

The main character lacks the necessary charisma for a leading role. Despite the promising initial scene, the film loses rhythm and interest.

In Mexico, some noteworthy westerns were shot, among them "El diabólico" (Giovanni Korporaal, 1977) , "El tunco Maclovio" (Alberto Mariscal, 1970) , "El Santo contra los jinetes del terror" (René Cardona, 1970) or the singular and misunderstood "El extraño hijo del sheriff" (Fernando Durán Rojas, 1982). Without forgetting one of the most famous contributions of the western to the Mexican: The lysergic "El Topo" (1970) by Alejandro Jodorowsky.

The director José Bolaños made in 1978 an adaptation of the novel "Pedro Páramo" by Juan Rulfo. But the best known film version of that book (and quite overrated, by the way) had been shot in 1967 by Carlos Velo.

Barbara Angely, who has a fleeting role at first as the mother of little Johnny, appears in the aforementioned "El tunco Maclovio".

The gravedigger Applebee is played by James Westerfield, veteran actor of classic westerns. This "Dead Aim" would be his last appearance in a movie. He died the same year as the film was shot, and he would never get to see it released.

El Diabólico

Mexico, 1977

Director: Giovanni Korporaal

Script: Giovanni Korporaal

Cast: Carlos East (Dave Boland), Jorge Humberto Robles (Oscar Peterson), Odila Flores (Eileen)

Plot

Oscar Peterson is a humble shoeshine boy in a wild west town. He is a shy individual, incapable of killing a fly and who has never touched a gun in his life. The men of the place mock him, and the women also cruelly ridicule him.

A fearsome masked outlaw is spreading terror in the region. The bandit arrives in Oscar's village, robbing a bank there. Not satisfied with robbing everything, he murders the clerk and kidnaps the banker's daughter, who was there. The criminal wears a medallion around his neck with a disturbing emblem; it looks like a satanic sign. That night the criminal rapes the girl, then marks the sinister symbol with a hot iron on her chest. The young woman, humiliated and badly wounded, is returned to the village, where she dies shortly afterwards. The girl's father swears revenge.

Meanwhile, the bandit visits his girlfriend, vedette Eileen, and sleeps with her. Other girls who have seen the stranger in the vicinity run to warn the sheriff and the other men, who catch the criminal and prepare to hang him.

The wretched Oscar looks on as the outlaw Dave Boland, robber, rapist and murderer, is about to be hanged. But the medallion that hangs around his neck with that strange and shining insignia, as well as the demonic eyes of the condemned man, radiate something that takes over Oscar's mind... An incredible thing happens then: The timorous and pusillanimous shoeshine man grabs the gun of another of the spectators and with one accurate shot cuts the rope that was going to hang the prisoner. The prisoner escapes with Oscar on a horse, and both are pursued by the people of the town. The bandit is wounded and realizes that his final moments have arrived. He then gives Oscar his medallion and makes him swear "by Satan" that he will avenge his death... Now Oscar will be the new "Diabólico".

His predecessor has revealed where he was hiding his loot, so Oscar gets several bags filled with huge amounts of gold nuggets, the result of countless robberies and pillages.

The men of the village find the body of the murderer, and the father of the girl raped by him requests that the body be hung from a tree branch to be devoured by vultures and coyotes. Oscar goes into the desert, followed by his old neighbors. When he runs out of provisions and water, he and his horse fall faintly into the burning sands. A young Indian girl discovers them, gives them something to drink and takes Oscar to her hut. There the new Diabólico is recovering, and decides to become a great gunman.

He asks his Indian friend (who is mute) to go and buy bullets with one of the nuggets of his booty as payment. The shop owner gives her the ammunition, but he wonders where the Indian girl got such a pure gold nugget... Oscar starts his shooting practice and his aim is more and more accurate. Meanwhile, the shop owner has warned some bandits to go to the mute squaw's hut in search of more gold. Imagining that something like this could happen, Oscar has taken the precaution of hiding the nuggets outside, burying them in the surroundings. The outlaws arrive and try to rape the Indian girl, but are liquidated by Oscar... who instead of untying his friend, blinded by the evil influence of the medallion, rapes her and then marks her symbol with the hot iron, as his predecessor used to do with the women he possessed...

Then Oscar puts the Indian woman to bed, says goodbye to her, takes the nuggets he had buried and goes back on his way. In another village he buys a black suit like the one Dave Boland wore, so he looks more and more like the old "Diabólico"...

While everybody is looking for him, while he is creating more and more enemies, the fugitive Oscar (as lonely as before but much more powerful) will be involved in several adventures, always betraying those who had trusted him: For a short time he is part of Arizona Jane´s gang, and then he sells her to the authorities and collects the reward... In a saloon Oscar will meet the old drunkard Hank, who reveals the location of a gold mine and proposes him to become a partner. When the precious metal has been discovered, Oscar kills the old man by crushing his head with a rock so as not to have to share the gold with him...

171

Oscar's fame as a dangerous criminal is growing throughout the region, while the body of Dave Boland, which is still hanging from the tree, is decomposing and becoming bare, the grass of vultures. A bounty hunter known as Colorado Kid, hired by the raped girl's father, will try to stop the evil Oscar and put an end to his misdeeds...

Commentary

This atypical western made in Mexico has interesting paranormal elements that could lead us to classify it as a crossover with the horror genre. The demonic power of the medallion and its cursed sign exercises a total influence on the personality of the one who wears it. The power of the "Diabólico" manages to overcome the limits between life and death by means of the evil amulet, since it serves to capture parasitic incorporeal entities that appropriate the human will. In this way, the naive and timid shoe-shiner Oscar was transformed overnight into a fearsome gunman, capable of the most aberrant monstrosities.

The film is directed by Giovanni Korporaal, of Dutch national but resident in Mexico throughout his career.

The elderly actor Victorio Blanco (1893-1977), who plays Hank, died the same year the film was released, this being one of his last works. In 1963 he had participated in "La maldición de la Llorona" (by Rafael Baledón) a classic of Mexican Gothic cinema.

El tren de la muerte ("The train of death")

Mexico, 1979

Director: Juan Orol

Script: Juan Orol

Cast: Julio Alemán (Álvaro Cortés), Patricia Rivera (Estela),
Víctor Manuel Mendoza (Sheriff), Arturo Martínez (Tony
López, the Mexican), Dinorah Judith (Vilma), Claudio Sorel
(Brooks)

Music: Ernesto Cortázar Jr.

Plot

A lonely stranger arrives by train in the village "Valle del
Paraíso" ("Paradise´s Valley"). He stays in the saloon run by
Vilma. There are often fights between members of two rival
gangs: The gangs of Tony the Mexican and Anselmo Martín.
The local sheriff tries to keep order and avoid disputes by
throwing those who are looking for trouble out of town.

The stranger's name is Álvaro Cortes. He has come to town in
search of Martín and his partner Marciano, with whom he wants
to settle a score on a matter of the past. Álvaro asks Estela, one
of the chorus girls in the saloon, if she knows where he can find
them. The girl says she doesn't know, but it's obvious that she
prefers to keep quiet out of fear.

Álvaro goes up to Vilma's office, and there he finds his old acquaintance Brooks. He has some unfinished business with him, too. After an exchange of shots, the stranger kills Brooks and for the time being is forced to look for accommodation elsewhere - for the town sheriff is now looking for him for murder.

Estela, the girl in the saloon, has had second thoughts and goes to look for Álvaro to tell him that she does know where he can find his enemies. She wants him, in exchange for his help, to take her away from that miserable town. However, Estela regrets her betrayal and goes to warn Martín and Marciano that a stranger is looking for them.

A group of gunmen attacks Álvaro as he heads for Marciano's ranch, but Vilma intervenes to save him. She explains later that she is not really the owner of the saloon, but that she serves as a "screen" and the real owner is the fearsome Marciano. Vilma also wants to escape from the village and asks the stranger to take her with him...

Commentary

This is Juan Orol's last film, shot when the Galician director was already 81 years old. The director's senescence is quite noticeable, since the film is made with an ineptitude that is even endearing. Too many dialogues, very unstable characters in their way of proceeding and intentions, confusing situations that lead nowhere, errors of continuity, notorious failures of rhythm...

This is the only Orolian contribution to the western genre (already completely out of fashion at that time). On many occasions, Mexican western films, or "chilli-western", were reminiscent of Italian versions of the genre from the '60s. But that is not the case here. "El tren de la muerte" is more reminiscent of the mediocre American westerns of the 1930s (I'm not saying that all American westerns of the 1930s were mediocre). Only in terms of the storyline, with a lonely stranger seeking revenge, the movie is somehow similar to the Italian style; but not at all in style or atmosphere.

Álvaro Cortés is played by an actor who is quite well known in Mexico (also involved in politics), and who stood out especially in the chilli-western subgenre. He is Julio Alemán, the protagonist of "El tunco Maclovio" (Alberto Mariscal, 1970).

Estela is embodied by a beautiful Patricia Rivera, who soon after would participate in "Perro callejero 2" (Gilberto Gazcón, 1981) - Mexican-style cinema about street kids. Vilma is characterized by Dinorah Judith, Orol's last muse and fifth wife (51 years younger than him) who we saw in the also very boring "Las pasiones infernales" (1969) or in the more entertaining "Historia de un gángster" (1969) and "Contrabandistas del Caribe" (1968) - Needless to say, all directed by Orol.

Printed in Great Britain
by Amazon